Making Noah's Ark Toys in Wood

Alan & Gill Bridgewater

 Sterling Publishing Co., Inc.   New York

In our research for this book, we have received the help and advice of a wide range of people from several different countries. But of them all, we would especially like to thank Pauline Cockrill, the museum assistant of the Bethnal Green Museum of Childhood in London, England, for her enthusiastic help.

Edited by Laurel Ornitz

Library of Congress Cataloging-in-Publication Data

Bridgewater, Alan.
     Making Noah's ark toys in wood / Alan and Gill Bridgewater.
          p.   cm.
     Includes index.
     ISBN 0-8069-6726-9 (pbk.)
     1. Wooden toy making.   2. Noah's ark.   I. Bridgewater, Gill.
II. Title.
TT174.5.W6B73 1988
745.592—dc19   88-21040
                                                                                        CIP

     3   5   7   9   10   8   6   4

Copyright © 1988 by Alan and Gill Bridgewater
Published by Sterling Publishing Co., Inc.
387 Park Avenue South, New York, N.Y. 10016
Distributed in Canada by Sterling Publishing
% Canadian Manda Group, P.O. Box 920, Station U
Toronto, Ontario, Canada M8Z 5P9
Distributed in Great Britain and Europe by Cassell PLC
Artillery House, Artillery Row, London SW1P 1RT, England
Distributed in Australia by Capricorn Ltd.
P.O. Box 665, Lane Cove, NSW 2066
Manufactured in the United States of America
All rights reserved
Sterling ISBN 0-8069-6726-9 Paper

Contents

Color section follows page 32.

Introduction

The Ark is a wonderful toy that has the power and quality of being all things to all children. In a child's fertile imagination, the Ark might become a proud and splendid Spanish galleon, a palace, a zoo full of roaring animals, a fort under siege, a well-stocked farm, a collection of priceless dolls—for a creative child, the play possibilities are limitless.

But perhaps more to the point, the Ark is all things to all woodworkers. No matter what your craft interests—be they cabinetmaking, joinery, wood carving, whittling, marquetry, stencilled folk design, wood turning, doll making, or naïve painting—the Ark, in its many and varied forms, can be modified to suit your own interests, skill levels, tools, techniques, and designs.

In times past, children in strict Victorian and

Illus. 1. This drawing is a copy of an illustration from the Girl's Own Book, written in 1853. Note the rather small size of the Ark, the roof skylight, the opening front door, and the simple, rounded-box type of boat.

5

Puritan households were forbidden to play with toys on Sundays. Playing with toys was regarded as being loose, a violation, or even sinful. Tired, work-worn parents would wag their fingers and tell their children, "The Devil finds work for idle hands" or "Remember the Sabbath to keep it holy." However, the parents thought that since the Noah story comes from the Bible, the Ark deserved special consideration. If the children were quiet and stayed in their room, then the Ark could be deemed a permissible Sunday amusement—not so much a toy, but more of a cautionary, scriptural, educational aid.

Every middle-class Victorian child knew by heart how—according to the Bible in Genesis, Chapters 6 and 7—God brought down a great flood that destroyed everything except for Noah; his wife; their three sons, Shem, Ham, and Japheth; the three sons' wives; and at least two of every kind of insect, beast, and bird. The children knew how Noah, his nearest and dearest, and all the animals escaped the great deluge by building a huge boat, or Ark, and how eventually the Ark came safely to rest on Mount Ararat in Armenia. This is certainly a fantastic story, and surely it must have been very tedious playing with the same old Ark every Sunday. But it wasn't tedious at all, at least not for Eleanor Acland who, in her evocative book, *Goodbye for the Present*, tells of her remembered Victorian childhood and of the fun she had with her Ark:

On Sunday, and on Sundays only, we played with our Noah's Ark, which during the rest of the week stood high and unheeded on the inaccessible Ararat of the very top bookshelf. It contained, besides Noah and his family, some eighty couples of animals and birds, very sketchily carved and coloured. Still, you could distinguish one breed from another readily enough. The elephants had trunks; the tigers and zebras, orange and black stripes respectively; the camels one hump; the dromedaries two. The horses had long tails; the giraffes, long necks. So that if all the animals' heads were almost, and their legs exactly, alike, what of it? . . . The humans also had a striking family resemblance. They had identical black eyes and eyebrows, scarlet mouths, and no noses; round heads and no necks. But the males wore straight-down garb, whereas the females were pinched in at the waist; and Noah and Mrs Noah had wider-brimmed hats than their sons and daughters-in-law. They suited us on Sundays, just as the brick people did on weekdays. We began our play with the traditional "animals went in two by two," and then branched off into variations on *Treasure Island* and *Swiss Family Robinson* . . . We secretly hoped and prayed for rain on Sundays, not only because that excused us from the boredom of church, but because we loved our Sunday occupations.

So there you have it. As far as our grandparents and great grandparents were concerned, the Ark wasn't an ordinary plaything, such as a hoop or a skipping rope; with its figures and 300, or so, animals, it was the biggest and the best Sunday toy of its day. And we do mean big—many were 36 inches from prow to stern, 18 inches wide, and up to 18 inches high, which made them physically very impressive.

It's believed that Arks were originally made in the wood-carving areas of Germany—first as one-of-a-kind toys, then as part of a cottage industry, and later becoming mass-produced. During the 250-year history of the Ark, its basic form has remained, more or less, unchanged. Traditionally, there was the house, which was usually carved and worked in the local style; there were the eight doll-like figures; and there were the hundred, or so, pairs of animals. The Ark house normally had two, or more, stories, walls decorated with folk patterns, doors and windows, birds on the roof, lace curtains, door knockers, a letter box, and roses around the door; and it was usually mounted on a boatlike base, complete with a prow, stern, and figurehead. As to how the figures and animals were packed into the Ark, usually either one wall slid back or the roof was hinged. As a finishing touch (and just to keep the children on their toes and to let them know what was in store for them if they got into mischief and disturbed the Sunday peace), cautionary verses were often pasted to the underside of the roof flap. One such verse goes:

God saw men's wicked ways
And nipped them in the bud,

He let it rain for forty days
And drowned them with a flood.
The bad all died, but mark!
God saved good Noah's life.
He saved him in a mighty Ark
With his three sons and wife.
And two of every kind
Of insect, beast and bird—
As He said, for you will find
God always keeps his word.
So now with you and me
Be this well understood—
If bad, we too shall punished be,
But blessed if we are good.
Anon.

Is it any wonder that Victorian children were seen and not heard?

As to construction and design, Arks were carved from solid baulks of wood, built up barrellike from staves, decorated with marquetry, stencilled, and so on. From Ark to Ark, the houses varied from Tyrolean cottages and German farmhouses to Pennsylvanian barns.

Just as the Ark houses were inspired by the houses of their makers, the animals and figures reflected the traditional craft skills of the areas where they were made. For example, in the Thuringian forest, the peasant toy makers whittled and carved Mr. and Mrs. Noah and dressed them in Thuringian folk costumes, and in the Erzgebirge area the figures and animals were both turned and carved. In America Mr. Noah wore side whiskers, a top hat, a watch and chain, and tails. Suffice it to say that traditional costume styles were as different and varied as those of their makers.

Now, as to how you should tackle the projects, you may be wondering if you need to start with the first project in the book and work relentlessly through each succeeding project. Although we have arranged the projects in an increasing order of complexity, you do not need to make them in any particular order. Each project has been carefully designed so that it can stand alone. If you only want to make the animals or the figures or whatever, then you can do so. Each project has its own inspirational, working, and detailed drawings, as well as its own instructions on tools and techniques. If the fancy strikes you, you can dip straight into the middle of the book and start with the project of your choice. But, if you want to start with the first project and work systematically through the book, then the carefully considered logical layout allows you to do so.

As you work through the projects, you will see that even though we have stayed within the tool-

Illus. 2. This is a copy of an illustration from a thirteenth-century manuscript showing Noah building the Ark under the direction of an angel. Note the classic boat form of the Ark.

Illus. 3. This is a drawing of a twentieth-century German Ark from the Staatliches Museum fur Volkskunst in Dresden, East Germany. Although the shapes have been simplified and varnished rather than painted, the Ark still contains all the usual details, such as the figurehead and the house.

8

and-technique spirit of a particular Ark-making tradition, we do suggest all manner of exciting variations and modifications. However, this doesn't mean that you should make each and every animal in a completely different way, but rather that you should consider all the tool-and-technique implications of the various approaches and then go for the approach that best suits your workshop, tools, and design abilities.

If you have any questions about the tools, materials, and techniques, the Glossary that follows should be especially helpful. With the book's well over 200 drawings and its no-stone-left-unturned step-by-step instructions, there is no reason why you shouldn't be able to make an Ark you can be proud of.

Even though many of the projects are relatively easy, each and every one presents a worthwhile challenge. If you want to make an authentic Ark for your children or grandchildren, show your students how to make a replica of a 200-year-old antique Ark, learn the secrets of making toys on the lathe, or bring back memories of childhood past, then this is the book for you.

Illus. 4. This is a copy of a drawing from a German toy-maker's catalogue, dated about 1840. Note all the beautifully worked details that have come to characterize German Arks—the figures in their brimmed hats, the stencilled roof, and the patterned band along the wall.

9

Glossary

Acrylics   Plastic polyvinyl-acetate-type paints that can be mixed with water or used straight from the can or tube. We favor such paints because they are simple to mix, they dry very quickly, and once dry they are completely waterproof.

Ark house   The houselike part of the Ark. It might actually be shaped like a house—with windows, doors, and a pitched roof—or it might be a square-topped box. Traditionally, Ark houses tended to reflect the architecture of their country of origin.

Arkite   Having to do with the Ark—for instance, the animals might be described as being arkite.

Ash   A long-grained tough wood—a good wood for making ring-turned animals.

Beech   A heavy, pleasant-to-carve inexpensive wood. It has a yellow sapwood and a reddish heart, and it's a good wood to use for wood turning.

Bench clamp   A screw device used for securing wood to the bench or for holding two, or more, pieces of wood together. It is also referred to as a clamp, cramp, G-clamp, or holdfast.

Berchtesgaden Ark   In the context of this book, a Berchtesgaden Ark is one that has been made in the small town of Berchtesgaden in southeast West Germany. The area has a living folk-art tradition of making wooden toys, which goes back at least to the fourteenth century. Berchtesgaden is to Ark toys as, say, Texas is to oil.

Blank   A block, slab, or disc of prepared wood.

Bobbin dolls   Small, doll-like, lathe-turned spindle forms that look as if they have a head, chest, and waist. A certain type of small clothespin might be described as a bobbin doll.

Brads   Small, delicate nails—it's best if they are headless, oval in section, and made from brass.

Brushes   Brushes come in all shapes and sizes. It's best to use good-quality artists' brushes for these projects. Be sure to wash them immediately after use and store them bristle-up.

Callipers   A two-legged compasslike instrument used for stepping off or transferring measurements.

Carcass   In the context of this book, the carcass is the framework, or structure, of the Ark, or the basic shell before it has been decorated and embellished.

Cardboard   A relatively stiff-bodied material made from rags or wood fibre. You might use special good-quality white cardboard for applied decorations, and cardboard from grocery boxes for building prototypes and making patterns.

Cartridge paper   A good-quality white or buff art paper. It's best to buy it flat, by the sheet.

Chuck   Any type of wood-holding device used on the lathe. A chuck might have three or four jaws or a central screw. Or, it might be the wood-turned hole type, meaning a dishlike form into which the wood is pushed.

Clamp   *See* Bench clamp.

Compass A two-legged instrument used for drawing circles and arcs. We recommend the long-legged screw-operated type.

Contact adhesive An easy-to-use, low-stress instant adhesive. First, you smear it on both surfaces, and then you bring the surfaces together.

Coping saw A frame saw used for cutting small sections of wood. The G-shaped frame allows you to easily fit and remove the thin flexible blades. It's a good saw to use for Ark making. Secure the work in a vise and hold the saw so that the blade passes through the wood at 90° to the working face (Illus. 5).

Craft knife and straightedge Working on a cutting board, hold the metal straightedge with one hand and carefully draw the knife towards you with the other. If you are worried about your fingertips, use a special metal M-section safety straightedge, available at crafts suppliers (Illus. 6).

Curved wood-carving tools Chisels and gouges with blades that are curved or shaped. They are used for digging, scooping, and hollowing out wood. You hold them in one hand and push them with the other, or bang them with a mallet.

Designing Working out a structure, pattern, or form by making sketches, outlines, models, or prototypes. It's a good idea to first research the subject by visiting such places as museums, galler-

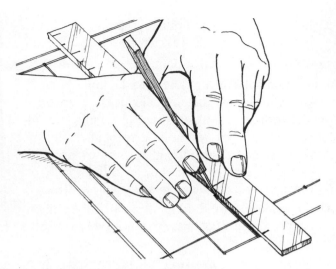

Illus. 6. A craft knife and a straightedge. Work with care, holding the straightedge with one hand and drawing the knife towards you with the other.

ies, and bookshops, and then draw the design to size.

Drilling holes Boring holes. It's best to use a small, inexpensive hand drill with a main grip handle, a large drive wheel, and a self-centering chuck.

Enamel paints Gloss-finished oil-based paints. Use those described as being nontoxic and lead-free, and make sure that they conform to current toy-safety standards. Always use the recommended primers, thinners, and undercoats, and be sure to clean your brushes immediately after use.

Erzgebirge Ark In the context of this book, an Erzgebirge Ark is one that has been made in and around the German towns of Grunhainichen, Seiffen, Olbernhau, and Marienberg. The whole area is famous for toy making, but especially for toys made on the lathe.

Faceplate A flat metal plate drilled for mounting the work. The faceplate is screwed onto the mandrel nose.

Filler Used for filling breaks and cavities. It's best to use a stable, two-tube car-body type of filler that can be sanded, sawed, and drilled.

Finishing Rubbing down, painting, decorating, varnishing, and otherwise enhancing the appearance of a project.

French straw-work Ark As made in Erzgebirge, Germany, this type of Ark is decorated with colored split-straw marquetry.

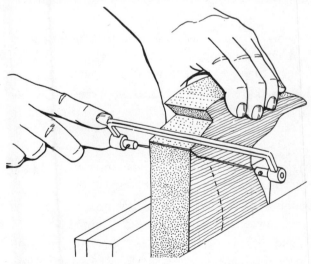

Illus. 5. A coping saw. A good saw for Ark making. Before you start a project, always make sure that you have plenty of spare blades.

11

Fretsaw   A fretsaw is similar to a coping saw, but it has a larger G-frame and finer, more fragile blades.

G-clamp   *See* Bench clamp.

Glues and adhesives   There are all kinds of glues and adhesives—from animal glues, rubber glues, and contact adhesives to hot glue guns, instant tube glues, and resins. We recommend using PVA (polyvinyl acetate) glue because it's easy to use, easily washed off when wet, not smelly or wasteful, and packaged in squeezable bottles.

Grain sealer   The fluid used to fill and block an open-grained wood prior to painting or varnishing.

Gridded working drawing   A scaled square grid placed over a working drawing. The object in the drawing can be reduced or enlarged, simply by changing the scale of the grid. For example, if the grid is described as one square to 1", and you want to double the scale, then all you do is make each square equal 2". When it's time to transfer the drawing to the wood, you just draw a grid to the suggested size and directly transfer the contents of each square. At one square to 1", you draw a full-size 1"grid; at two squares to 2", you draw a full-size 2" grid, and so on (Illus. 7).

Hammer   You need to use a small 4 oz. ash-handled hammer.

Hand drill   *See* Drilling holes.

Headstock   The casting on the left-hand end of the lathe (the end that is driven) that carries the spindle, or mandrel.

Holdfast   *See* Bench clamp.

Holly   A beautiful, close-grained, ivory-white wood that carves and turns well and takes fine details.

Inspirational material   In this book, the illustrations gathered on zoo, museum, and gallery visits are described as being inspirational.

Keyhole saw   A small knifelike saw used for making interior cutouts in large sheets—cutouts that are inaccessible to a coping saw or fretsaw. A keyhole saw is also called a pad saw.

Knife   You need to have a selection of knives at your disposal. If a small kitchen knife does the job, then it's the one to use.

Lathe   A woodworking machine in which the

Illus. 7. A means of reducing or enlarging an illustration. See how by transferring the contents of the small squares to squares that are twice as large, it is possible to double the size of the image.

workpiece is turned about a horizontal axis against a hand-held tool. For the projects in this book, it's best to use a small, power-driven lathe.

Lime wood   A close-grained, knot-free wood that is easy to work and can be cut and carved in almost any direction. The perfect wood for beginners.

Mallet   A wooden-headed hammer that is used primarily with a chisel or gouge.

Maquette   A working model, which can be made of clay, Plasticine, cardboard, or scrap wood.

Marking out   Making crisp, clear lines using a clean ruler and a pencil with a sharp point (Illus. 8). Don't forget the traditional woodworker's adage: "It's best to measure twice and cut once."

12

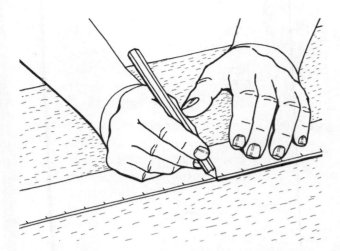

Illus. 8. Marking out. Check your measurements twice and only cut once.

Masking tape   A tape used for masking around areas that are to be painted or for securing paper to the drawing board. Don't use plastic tape.

Measure   A wooden ruler, tape measure, or steel ruler. It's best to use a steel ruler because it can also be used as a cutting edge.

Modifying   Changing or redesigning a project in terms of such variables as size, materials, and decorations. Or, changing details to suit your own preferences or needs.

Multi-ply   A close-grained, white, smooth-faced, superior-quality plywood, made up from thin 1/16" veneer layers. A 1/4"-thick sheet of multi-ply should be made up from four or five layers.

Nails   It's best to use brass brads, nails, or screws. Drive the head well into the wood and fill the hole. Make sure that the inside of the Ark is free from any nail points.

Naïve art   A term used to describe primitive, unsophisticated, uninhibited, traditional, self-taught, innocent folk art. Also used to describe designs, motifs, and forms of artistic and craft expression that have to do with ordinary folk.

Nurnberg   A German toy-making town, traditionally known for the production of tin soldiers and wood-carved figures.

Off cuts   Bits and pieces (remnants) of scrap wood that can be saved and used at a later date.

Pad saw   *See* Keyhole saw.

Painted decoration   Made by using a good-quality,

fine-point brush. Load the brush with paint and then let the natural shape and fall of the brush guide your strokes (Illus.9).

Paints and painting   Before painting, always clear away bench clutter, wipe up dust, arrange a drying line or rack, and set up your tools and materials so that they will be conveniently close at hand. Having selected primers, undercoats, and top coats that are compatible (you might use acrylics, enamels, model maker's colors, or homemade milk paints), and remembering to let the paint dry out between coats, apply the primer, undercoat, top ground color, details, and varnish.

Parquetry   Similar to wood-veneer marquetry, but the designs are geometrical.

Peasant tradition   *See* Naïve art.

Pencils   You need a good selection of pencils on hand. We recommend using soft 2Bs for designing and tracing, and hard Hs for press-transferring. Beware of using alcohol-based felt-tip markers since they stain and bleed through paints.

Piercing saw   A small G-frame saw that is similar to the coping saw and fretsaw. The piercing saw takes fine blades and short pieces of broken blade.

Plasticine   A modelling material used for making models, prototypes, and maquettes.

Primer   A special type of base paint used for filling, protecting, and sealing. Wood primers are full-bodied enough to block out stains and rough

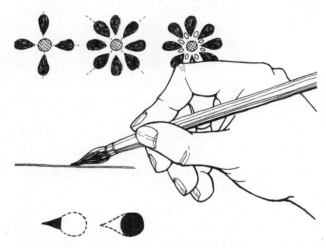

Illus. 9. Painting. You need a good selection of broad and fine-point brushes. Buy the best and wash them after you use them.

grain. Make sure that your sealers, primers, undercoats, and top coats are compatible; when in doubt, ask your supplier.

Profile A form, blank, or cutout. This term is also used to describe the flat silhouette, or side view.

Prototype The initial model made prior to buying and cutting your wood. You might make figure prototypes from Plasticine, and Ark prototypes from cardboard and tape or from inexpensive throwaway wood.

PVA glue Polyvinyl acetate glue—a white, easy-to-use woodworking glue.

Reinforced carton-sealing tape Brown or white paper tape for parcels—a lick-and-stick tape with a water-based glue or adhesive.

Resin glue A two-tube resin-to-hardener adhesive. It needs to be used with care; always read the instructions.

Riffler files Small, shaped files that are used for working small corners, holes, and curves.

Rivet In the context of this book, a rivet is an easy-to-use, soft-headed metal fastener that is used to pivot-attach two, or more, pieces of wood.

Rivet gun An inexpensive tool used to snap-attach the heads of rivets.

Rubbing down Rubbing the wood down with a series of graded sandpapers to achieve a smooth, ready-to-paint finish.

Sanding sticks Shaped pieces of wood, plastic, or bone that can be used to support sandpaper. A plastic spoon, an old comb, and a lollipop stick, all make good sanding sticks.

Sandpaper An abrasive used in the rubbing-down process. Sandpaper is purchased in graded packs and used in a rough-to-smooth order. Sanding is a pleasurable but dusty task that is best carried out well away from the painting and designing area.

Saxony A region in southeast Germany around the upper Elbe River that is famous for making wooden toys and Arks.

Scale The ratio between the working drawing and the model to be made. For example, if the scale is one grid square to 1", then you draw a full-size 1" grid and transfer the contents of the working-

drawing squares to your full-size squares. *See* Gridded working drawing.

Scalpel A slim-handled, fine-point razor-sharp knife used for cutting cardboard and paper and for carving and whittling fine details.

Scissors You need a pair of small sharp scissors. When cutting, move the paper so that the scissors are always presented with the line of the next cut. Try to keep your cutting smooth and even (Illus. 10).

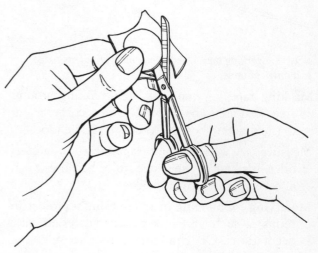

Illus. 10. Scissors. Guide the paper so that the scissors are always presented with the line of the next cut.

Seiffen An area in Germany that is famous for its tin and wood-carved toys.

Skew chisel A wood-turning and wood-carving tool that has a blade with an angled edge.

Skittle turning A simple, doll-like, between-center turning.

Small tree wood A section through a small tree—a tender, easy-to-work green wood.

Stave- or cooper-built In the context of this book, a term used to describe an Ark that has been built the same way as a barrel—that is, from a number of staves, or slats, that fit together edge to edge to make the total form.

Stencilling A technique used for applying a pattern or design to a surface (Illus. 11). With design windows, for example, cut out the shape in a sheet of cardboard, tape the cardboard plate to the object you are decorating, dab paint through the

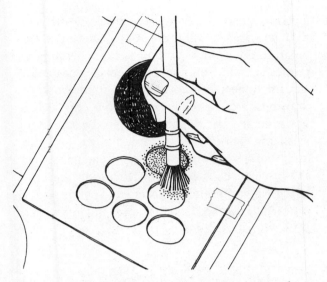

Illus. 11. Stencilling. Dab the paint through the stencil-plate "windows" with a crisp up-and-down movement.

cut-out cardboard windows onto the object with a semidry brush, and then carefully remove the plate.

Straight saw Just about any straight-bladed, fine-toothed woodworking saw—a tenon or a gents, for example.

Tailstock The right-hand side of the lathe—an adjustable live or dead point that you can easily slide along the bed of the lathe.

Template A pattern or cutout made of wood, plastic, or cardboard—a shape that is used to reproduce a number of identical shapes.

Thuringia A forested mountainous region in central East Germany that is famous for its wood-carved toys and Arks.

Tool rest A horizontal bar for supporting a hand tool that can be moved back and forth along the lathe bed. Adjust the tool rest and lock it in position so that its upper edge is slightly lower than the central axis of the wood being worked.

Tracing paper A strong translucent paper used for tracing. We usually work out a good design, take a tracing with a soft 2B pencil, line in the reverse side of the tracing, and then use a hard pencil to press-transfer the lines of the design through to the working face of the wood.

Undercoat A flat coat of paint that is applied to the workpiece after the primer and before the

gloss coat. Ideally, the workpiece should be primed, have two undercoats and a top coat, and be varnished.

Varnish In the context of this book, we are referring to a clear or golden yacht varnish. It can be brushed on, or the work can be dipped.

V-board Also called a V-table or a bird's-mouth fretsaw table. It is clamped to the work surface so that the V-notch extends beyond the surface. You must do the sawing near the vertex of the V-notch.

V-gouge Also called a veiner, it is used for carving fine V-section cuts, or trenches.

Vise A bench-mounted clamp that is available in all shapes and sizes. There are engineers' vises, all-wood vises, carvers' chops, and so on. The vise must be strong enough for the job at hand.

Whittling Cutting and carving with a small hand-held knife. Also refers to a simple, naïve folk carving. Use a comfortable-to-hold, sharp-edged knife, and work with a careful thumb-paring action (Illus. 12).

Workbench Regardless of whether you use a specially designed carpenter's bench or a strong kitchen table for a workbench, it needs to be strong enough to take a variety of clamps.

Working drawing A scaled and detailed drawing that includes sizes, sections, details, colors, moving parts, a cutting list, and so on. Never cut the original drawing; always take a tracing.

Illus. 12. Whittling. You need a couple of sharp whittling knives. Always work with carefully considered and controlled cuts, and be ready to stop immediately if you feel the blade running out of control.

Working face The best side of the wood—the side on which you draw the shapes and the outside of the Ark.

Work-out paper Inexpensive paper as might be used for initial roughs and work-out drawings. It's best to use a slightly matt white paper.

Workshop In the context of this book, your workshop can be just about any place from a spare room to a garden shed to the garage. Ideally, the room needs to have a workbench, a sink with warm running water, a power supply, good ventilation, plenty of shelf space, a heater, a bin for rubbish, a corner set aside for rubbing down, and a painting area. If you are a beginner, we suggest that you start with the basic space and then organize the surfaces and areas as the work progresses and you come to understand your needs. You might decide, for example, to do the working drawings in the kitchen or bedroom, the sawing in the garage, the rubbing down in the garden or yard, the painting in a garden shed, and the assembling back in the kitchen. Remember that sawdust can be hazardous, sharp tools are best kept away from small children, and paints sometimes give off toxic fumes. So, organize your workshop accordingly.

1
THE PENNSYLVANIAN ARK

The Pennsylvanian Ark (Illus. 13, and Illus. 1 on page A in the color section) is special, not because it is in any way wonderfully built or dramatically decorated, but rather because it has come to represent all the naïve wood-carved toys that we now associate with the American folk-art tradition.

Most likely the first Pennsylvanian Arks were made by Pennsylvanian German toy makers who drew their ideas from old-world designs. But it wasn't long before local carvers, woodworkers, and cabinetmakers began to introduce their own ideas, reshaping traditional German designs and techniques to suit their own needs. No doubt finding toy making to be pleasant and profitable work alongside cabinetmaking and chair making, they soon modified what they considered to be rather showy and overworked designs and built Arks that we now recognize as being uniquely sturdy in structure and naïve in design.

The local toy makers created Arks that were bold and direct and completely uncluttered by "hackneyed" old-world imagery. Most of these rural toy makers had never actually seen an elephant, a giraffe, or a camel, or any other exotic animal—nor were they familiar with classical painting or prints of exotic Arks or animals. And so it was that American Arks—which looked as if their inspiration was drawn from Indian dugout canoes, pioneer rafts, and Pennsylvanian German barns—came to house such fantastic animals as giraffes that looked like spotted horses and kangaroos that looked like dogs.

Illus. 13. The Pennsylvanian Ark. Even though this Ark has many old-world characteristics, the house, the boat, and the designs have been simplified to their most basic essentials. The Ark is about 16" long, 10" high, and 6" wide.

Project 1
Making an Ark in the Pennsylvanian Tradition

Working Out Your Structure and Design

Before you start building this particular type of Ark, take a good look at all the accompanying illustrations and consider all the tools, techniques, and materials that are required for the project.

Note how the Pennsylvanian Ark (Illus. 13) is less decorative and consequently easier to paint than the Berchtesgaden Ark (Illus. 52 on page 49), and see how its structure is smaller, more direct, and altogether less complex than that of the Cremer Ark (Illus. 131 on page 124); then consider how these characteristics are perhaps outweighed by the fact that its flat raftlike base needs to be carved rather than box-built. Certainly, the carving is relatively easy and straightforward, but you'll need a stout woodworking bench and a selection of woodcarving gouges to do it.

Study the cutting grid (Illus. 14) and see how, at one grid square to 1", the Ark is about 16" long from prow to stern, 10" high, and 6" wide. In Illus. 15, note how the Ark's beautifully simple and direct design makes this project especially easy for beginners. For example, one side of the roof swings up on four very ordinary functional strap hinges. You don't need to bother with setting the hinges into the wood or screwing them on the underside since they are screwed directly onto the roof. And so it is with the curvy strip of dado decoration that runs around the edge of the roof—it hasn't been painstakingly traced and outlined, but simply worked from a strip of folded and cut paper and then mounted directly. This straightforward, easy-to-work approach is also taken with the windows and doors—which are cut out of thin cardboard, painted, and then mounted directly onto the walls—and with the swags under the windows—which are worked with a center-line stencil. Also, notice how the boat-shaped base has been worked from a length of plank wood, angled at the prow and stern, relief-carved at both ends, and bevelled on the underside edge.

When you have studied all the drawings and considered making certain modifications, try to see

On the following pages: Illus. 14 (left). Cutting grid. The scale is one grid square to 1". Illus. 15 (right). Working drawing. Top: The scale is one grid square to 1". Note the window, foliage, and dado templates, and the carved-boat section.

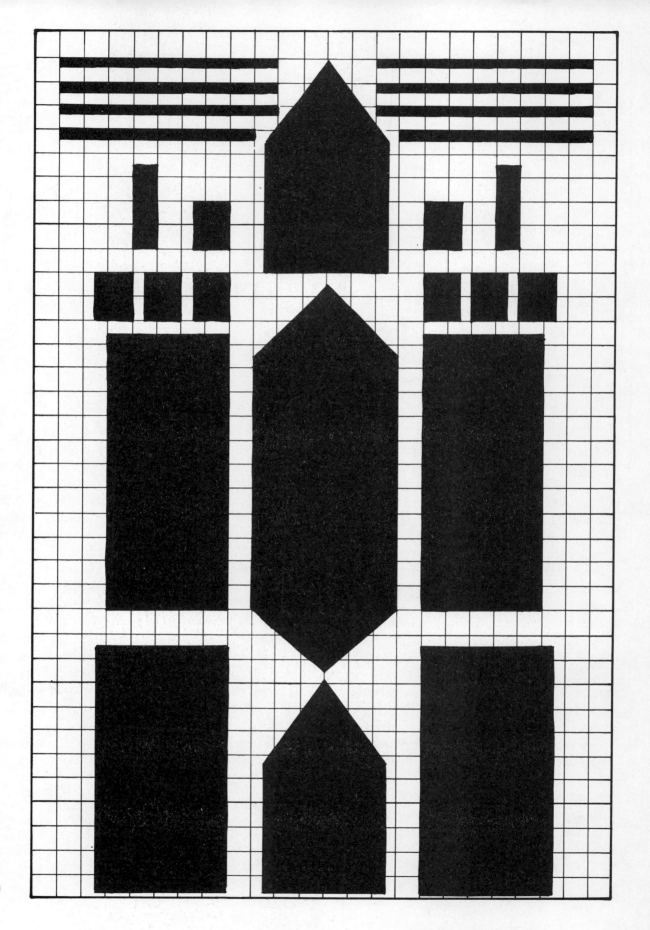

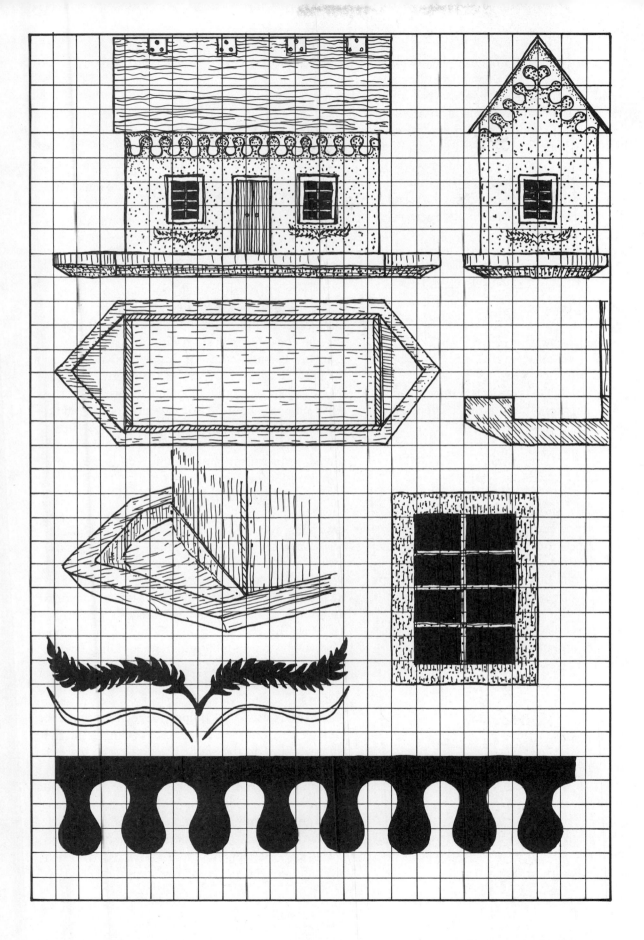

as many Arks as possible. Of course, take a look at classic Arks—meaning those made in Germany, England, and Switzerland—but focus your attention on those Arks that were made in America between about 1810 and 1900. When you have analyzed what it is that makes American folk-art Arks so special, sit down with a pad of work-out paper and a pencil, and make a number of sketches. Finally, with gridded paper and a pencil and ruler, draw a full-size working design, complete with front, side, and plan views.

Tools and Materials

For this project you need:
- a piece of 1"-thick plank wood that is 16" long and 6" wide for the base;
- a piece of ¼"-thick wood that is about 72" long and 6" wide for the house;
- about 72" of ¼ X ¼" square wood (or you can use remnants) for strengthening the inside angles;
- a straight saw;
- a selection of straight and curved wood-carving tools, including a small straight chisel, a V-section tool, and a U-section gouge;
- a small mallet;
- a small amount of cardboard or thin plywood for the doors and windows;
- a sheet of superior-quality white cartridge paper for the decorative dado strip;
- four small strap hinges, either decorative and made of brass or functional and made of mild steel;
- screws to fit the hinges;
- wood primer and undercoat;
- a selection of acrylic paints;
- brushes;
- a sponge;
- scissors;
- a screwdriver;
- a hammer;
- a quantity of brads or nails, preferably made of brass;
- PVA glue;
- contact adhesive;
- a bench clamp;
- a Surform rasp;
- a pack of graded sandpapers;

- a measure;
- a square; and
- a craft knife or scalpel.

Cutting and Carving the Boat-Shaped Base

Take a good look at all your wood, just to make sure that it is completely free from knots, stains, sappy edges, and splits. Pin up your designs and drawings so that they are within view, and arrange your tools so that they are close at hand.

Now, set the 16"-long piece of 1"-thick slab wood, face up, on the bench, and mark out the position of the prow, the stern, and the two triangular relief-carved sunken areas—the pulpit at the prow and the cockpit at the stern. Establish a center line that runs the full length of the plank. Noting that the prow is slightly sharper than the stern, mark out the wood accordingly. The angled cutback of the prow starts at about 3" from the end of the plank, whereas that of the stern starts at about 2½". Use a measure and square to establish these points, and then draw lines from the side points to the prow and stern ends of the center line.

When you have marked out the plank and double-checked to make sure it's correct, use the straight saw to cut away the four triangular pieces of waste. Now, take the rasp and sandpaper, and work the sawn points at the prow and stern to a smooth finish. When this is done, measure about ¾" to 1" in from the sides of the plank and mark out a border that runs right around the boat shape; use this margin to establish the triangular pits. To avoid confusion, label the boat ends *prow* and *stern*, and shade in the areas that need to be recessed.

Now, secure the plank to the bench with the clamp and set out your carving tools. Take the small V-tool and outline the pulpit and cockpit triangles. Cut a V-section trench around the triangles, all the time working on the waste side and keeping about ⅛" away from the drawn lines. Bearing in mind that you are cutting both with and across the grain of the wood, hold the tool firmly with both hands—one hand guiding and the other pushing and maneuvering. Working to a uniform depth of about ¼", try to cut a smooth trench. Once you have trenched around both triangles, take a small straight chisel or a gouge with a shallow U-section, and position the tool so that the blade is on the drawn line; angle the handle so that it is over the border and then work around the triangle with a series of short, sharp taps of the mallet (Illus. 16). As you chop, the band of waste between the drawn line and the V-trench should crumble away. Once the drawn lines have been set in, use a shallow-curve gouge and start to clear away the waste to a depth of about ¼". As far as possible, work across or at an angle to the grain, using the V-trench depth as a guide. Don't try to dig out great clumps of wood, but rather settle for removing small crisp curls. Once you have wasted and lowered both triangles to about ¼", repeat the process, aiming for a straight-sided, flat-based finished depth of about ½".

When this is done, turn the flat boat shape over and use the rasp to cut back and bevel the underside edges. Finally, take the graded sandpapers and rub the wood down to a smooth splinter-free finish.

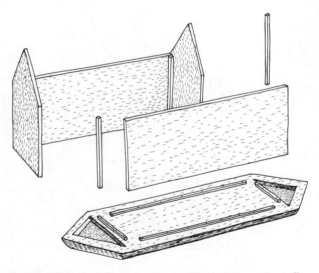

Illus. 17. Glue and nail the four walls, and strengthen all inside angles with small section strips bedded in glue.

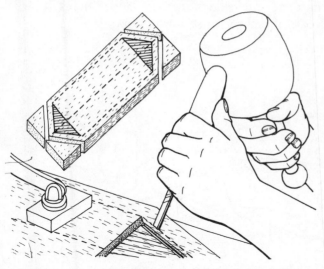

Illus. 16. Position the blade on the drawn line, angle the handle so that it is over the border, and then make a series of short, sharp taps. Note how the wood is secured with a bench holdfast.

Building the House

Take a look at the illustrations, and notice how the gabled walls at the ends of the house sit flush with the sides of the recessed triangles, whereas the long walls are set ¾" to 1" back from the sides of the boat. Then use a measure, a square, and a straight saw to

cut out the wood for the house. You need six boards in all: two for the gabled walls, at about 5" wide and 9" high; two for the long walls, at about 10 ½" long and 5 ½" high; and two for the roof, at about 11 ½" long and 5" wide.

It's best to cut the gabled walls first, and then to shape and adjust the other pieces to fit. Glue and nail the long walls onto the edges of the gabled walls. Once you have established the four-wall shell and have made sure that it is reasonably square and upright, use the ¼" X ¼" section strips and the glue and nails to strengthen the inside angles and to fit and attach the house onto the flat deck of the boat (Illus. 17).

Having made sure that the two roof boards are a good fit and finish, hinge them along the ridge edge. Finally, dribble a little glue on one slope of the gabled walls, carefully position the hinged-roof boards, and then attach them with nails or brads (Illus.18).

Windows, Doors, Dadoes, and Window Swags—Paper Cutting, Painting, and Finishing

Look at the drawings, and see how the windows and doors are worked from cardboard (we could have used plywood). Note that the windows are 1½" wide and 2" high, and that the doors are a little under 2" wide and a fraction over 3" high. Then carefully

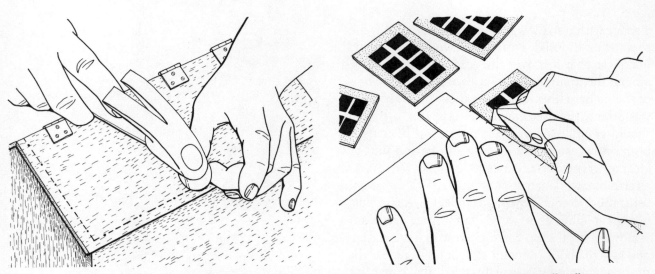

Illus. 18 (left). Hinge the roof boards along the ridge. Glue and nail one half of the roof to the top of the walls. Illus. 19 (right). Once you have painted the cardboard windows, use a craft knife and a metal straightedge to cut them out.

measure, mark, and cut the cardboard accordingly. On the windows, use a pencil and ruler to mark out the bars and the surrounding areas (Illus. 19).

When it comes to making the cut-paper under-the-roof dado, cut the white cartridge paper into 1"-wide strips and then carefully mark out and zigzag, or fanfold, it so that you have a working face that measures 1" high and about ³/₈" wide. When this is done, mark out the half S-shape; then, a few folds at a time, work through the folded strip, cutting out the "tongue" forms (Illus. 20). You need to work about 50" of strip.

After you have cut and worked the dado comes the pleasurable task of putting it all together. Remembering to let the paint dry out between coats, apply a primer, an undercoat, and the top coat to the Ark. See how we have used bold bright colors—red for the roof, blue for the house, brown for the boat, black for the window panes, green for the doors, and so on (refer to Illus. 1 on page A in the color section). Paint the Ark inside and out and then put it aside to dry.

When the paint is completely dry, mark out the position of the windows, the door, and the dado strip, and then attach the door and the windows with the contact adhesive. Working on a clean surface, brush the back of the paper dado with water and PVA glue, wait a while for the paper to stretch and settle, and then carefully arrange it around the top edge of the walls and gables.

Now, mark in the window swags with a stencil and highlight the details with a little white paint (Illus. 21). Once the paint and glue are dry, sign and date the underside of the boat, and then apply two coats of yacht varnish to the workpiece.

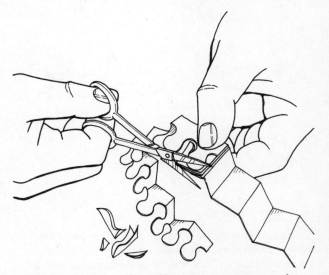

Illus. 20. Working a few folds at a time, use a pair of scissors to cut out the "tongue" form.

Troubleshooting and Possible Modifications

• Instead of having the roof hinges show, you can fit them on the underside. Either way, make sure

24

that you place them so that the roof flap can be folded right back.

• If you are put off by the idea of cutting and gluing the windows, doors, and dado, you might prefer using paint and stencils.

• You can modify the project by either building the boat shape up from layers of plywood, or by adding a smooth one-level deck running right through from prow to stern and then edging the deck with a beading.

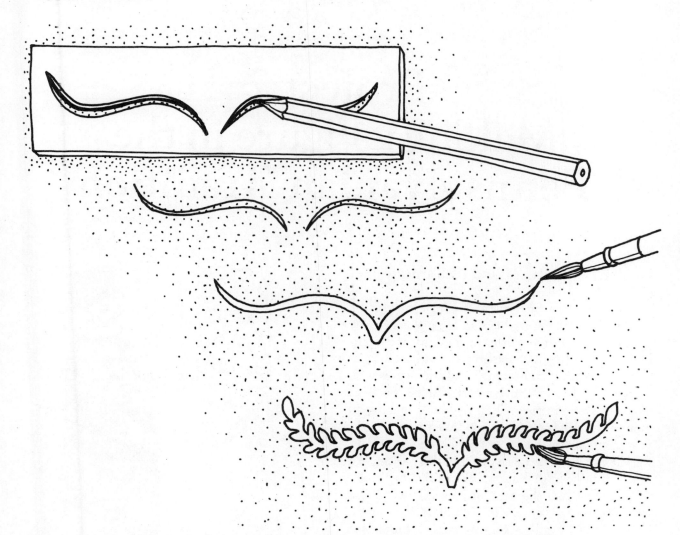

Illus. 21. From top to bottom: Pencil in the stencil "window," remove the stencil plate, paint in the pencil-drawn shape, and then add the foliage details with a fine-point brush.

Project 2
Making a Figure in the Pennsylvanian Tradition

Design, Structure, and Technique Considerations

Although many Pennsylvanian toy makers closely followed traditional European designs and techniques, some began to experiment with new ideas and methods. Of course, making little figures with swinging arms wasn't such an original idea because, after all, German toy makers had been making all manner of moving figures and Ark toys for many years. But making figures out of plywood and pivoting their arms on metal rivets, as in this project, was a new American invention (Illus. 22).

Who first had the idea, and exactly when and where such toys were made, are now almost impossible to say. Certainly, Charles Crandall, the famous American toy maker, was making his jointed figures and animals as early as 1867; but as to how long before that date such figures were being made, no one knows for sure. But, no matter—as far as we are concerned, it's not so much the when and where that counts, but the how.

Now, take a good look at the working drawings (Illus. 23 and 24), and notice how these charming figures—which were obviously inspired by much earlier European Ark figures—have certain characteristics that are evocative of nineteenth-century American traits and styles. Mrs. Noah—with her

Illus. 22. Project picture. Worked in 1/8"-thick multi-ply and standing about 4" high, these figures have swinging arms attached with rivets.

26

bustle, bun, and beautiful straight back—and Mr. Noah—with his broadcloth coat, full prosperous figure, and square-cut beard—might well have stepped right out of a comfortable mid-nineteenth-century Pennsylvanian drawing room. Also, see how the figures are built up from 1/8"-thick multi-ply. The body and the arms are made from a single-plywood thickness, there are brass washers between the wood layers and the ends of the pop rivets, and the base is built up, or laminated, from three pieces of plywood. Note how, at four grid squares to 1", the figures are about 4" high.

Study all of the accompanying drawings, and when you have a good understanding of how the project needs to be worked, spend time with a pencil and work-out paper and decide whether you want to copy our designs exactly or make your own modifications. For example, you might want to change the period and have the figures dressed in early American Pilgrim costumes; or, you might want to design the figures so that they resemble people in your family. Consider all the possibilities and then draw your chosen design profiles to size.

Tools and Materials

For this project you need:
- a sheet of 1/8"-thick multi-ply, at about 6" X 6";
- wooden matchsticks;
- the use of a pop rivet gun;
- long-headed rivets to fit the gun;
- four brass or white metal washers to fit the rivets;
- a coping saw (or a fretsaw);
- a pack of spare saw blades;
- a hand drill with a bit to suit the rivets;
- a pack of graded sandpapers;
- a pencil and measure;
- work-out paper;
- the use of a workbench;
- G-clamps;
- tracing paper;
- a selection of acrylic paints;
- broad and fine-point brushes;
- PVA glue;
- primer and undercoat; and
- all the usual workshop items, such as newspaper, cloths, and paint containers.

Setting Out the Design and Making Your First Cuts

When you have made a good workable design, take a careful tracing. Then, arranging the forms to make the best use of your available material, press-transfer the traced lines with a hard pencil through to the working face of your plywood (Illus. 25).

When this is done, take the wood and clamp it to the workbench. Being sure that the area that you want to fret out is hanging over the edge of the bench, take your saw and cut out the profiles (Illus. 26). As you are working, try not to twist the blade or apply too much pressure. Work at an even pace, all the while making sure that you cut on the waste side of the drawn lines and keep the blade at right angles to the working face. You also need to watch out that you don't rip or splinter the wood.

Working the Pivot and Mortise Holes

Take the cut pieces and set them out on the workbench. There should be six cutouts in all: the main body, the two arms, and the three base rectangles.

Now, starting with the body but also working the two arms, establish the precise position of the pivotal holes; then take the hand drill and the rivet-sized drill bit, and bore the three holes out—one in each of the two arms and one in the body. After you have made sure that the holes are well placed, slide a matchstick, or something similar, through the body and arms and go through a trial run to see how the arms will look.

Referring back to various drawings, see how the base is built up from three rectangles. Except for the top two pieces of ply each being worked with a mortise hole, the three pieces are identical. Now, take the two top pieces of wood and check to be sure

On the following pages: Illus. 23 (left). Working drawing for Mrs. Noah. The scale is about four grid squares to 1". Note the washer-wood-washer-wood-washer arrangement at the rivet point, and see how the 3/8"-thick base is built up from three 1/8"-ply thicknesses. Illus. 24 (right). Working drawing for Mr. Noah. The scale is about four grid squares to 1". Although we suggest using 1/8"-thick plywood for the body and building up the base from three plywood layers, there's no reason why you couldn't modify the details and use, for example, a thicker ply.

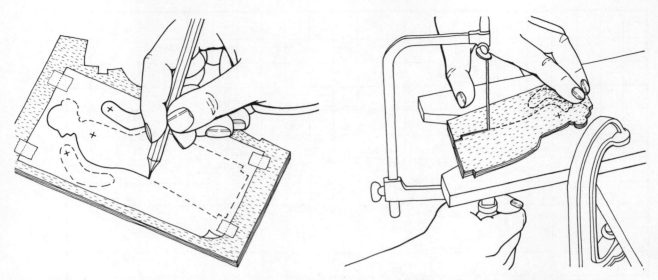

Illus. 25 (left). Secure the tracing with tabs of masking tape, and then use a hard pencil to press-transfer the traced lines through to the wood. Illus. 26 (right). Secure the plywood so that the line of cut is hanging over the V-board. Then use your chosen saw to fret out the form, working slightly on the waste side of the drawn line.

that the position and size of their base holes match up with the position and size of the tenon on the base of the figure. Next, secure the wood, a piece at a time, in the vise, and drill two blade-starting holes, one at each end of the slot. Now, dismantle the coping saw or fretsaw, pass the blade through one of the holes, locate and retension the blade in its frame, and then cut out the enclosed shape (Illus. 27). Bearing in mind that you will have to remove the blade from its frame four times, twice for each of the two base pieces, it's best to have the teeth of the blade pointing towards the handle so that you can cut on the pulling stroke.

Sanding and Painting

Once you have drilled a pivot hole in each of the two arms and the body, and have cut the two base slots, go through a trial run of putting it all together. Slide a matchstick through the body and the arms (again), and place the body tenon in the base slot (Illus. 28). The arms should swing on either side of the body profile, and the body tenon should pass through the two plywood base plates.

Now, dismantle the figure and work through the pack of graded sandpapers, rubbing the wood down to a smooth finish. All edges, corners, and holes need to be absolutely smooth and free from jags and rough areas. When this is done, clear away all the

dust and clutter and use a damp cloth to wipe down your working surface and the items to be painted.

Bearing in mind that you need to lay on a primer, an undercoat, a top coat, small details, and a final coat of varnish, and that the paint needs to dry and be rubbed down between coats, give some thought to your work area. If possible, it's a good idea to set aside a special area for painting. Once you have organized the painting area and decided how you are going to support the wood after it has been painted—that is, are you going to hang it on threads or spike

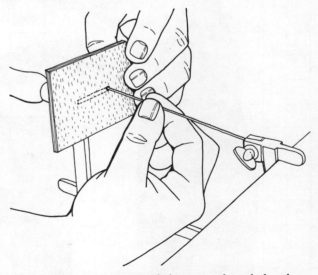

Illus. 27. Unhitch the saw blade, pass it through the pilot hole, and then secure the blade and re-tension.

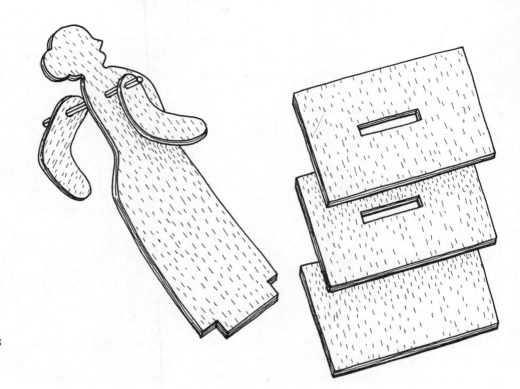

Illus. 28. Put all the pieces together and check for a good fit.

it on wires?—set out your brushes and paints (Illus. 29).

You may want to paint Mrs. Noah's dress a deep plum red, her collar white, her hands and face a flesh pink, and her hair a yellow-gold. The details of her dress and face can be painted with a black/brown.

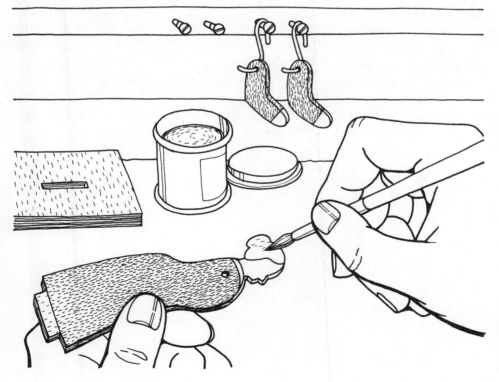

Illus. 29. Prior to painting, organize a drying area. You can use screws and bent wire to make a drying frame.

Refer to Illus. 1 on page A in the color section for some ideas on how to paint Mr. Noah. Finally, when the paint is dry and you have made sure that all the holes are clear and clean-edged, apply a coat of varnish and put the pieces to one side.

Putting the Parts Together and Finishing

Set out the six pieces of wood that make up the figure, the PVA glue, the blind rivet, the four washers to fit the rivet, and the rivet gun. With the handles of the rivet gun set wide apart, take the rivet and slide the naillike point, or mandrel, into the gun hole until the head of the rivet touches the nozzle.

Now, with the wooden shapes and the washers layered in the correct order—there should be a washer, an arm, another washer, the body, another washer, the other arm, and finally, another washer—insert the rivet through the sandwich and squeeze the handles of the gun together (Illus. 30). As you squeeze the handles, the head of the rivet should deform and the mandrel should snap off. However, if the rivet is slightly too long and the point doesn't snap off, pull the handles apart, slide the gun towards the head of the rivet, and take a second bite. The arms should have a tight swing fit.

Now, take the figure, dribble a small amount of glue on its tenon, and then carefully slide it into one of the two pierced-base pieces. Next, glue on the other pierced-base piece and then the solid piece.

Finally, rub down any rough corners or edges, touch up any scuffed areas with paint and varnish, and then begin making your next figure.

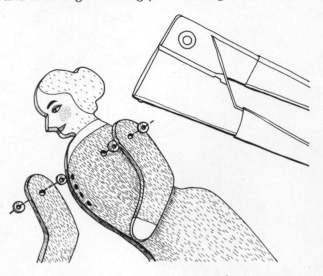

Illus. 30. When the paint is dry, make sure the holes are free from blobs of paint, check the wood-washer-wood-washer arrangement of the arms, and then rivet up.

Troubleshooting and Possible Modifications

• You might use thicker plywood, such as $3/16''$ or $1/4''$.

• When you buy the plywood, only select white multi-ply with the best face, that is plywood made from thin veneers. Avoid coarse-centered "stout heart" plywood—it's very difficult to work.

• When you buy the rivets, bear in mind that they need to pass through four washers and three layers of $1/8''$ plywood.

Illus. I. The Pennsylvanian Ark (pages 17–47)

A

Illus. 2. The Berchtesgaden Ark (pages 48–84)

B

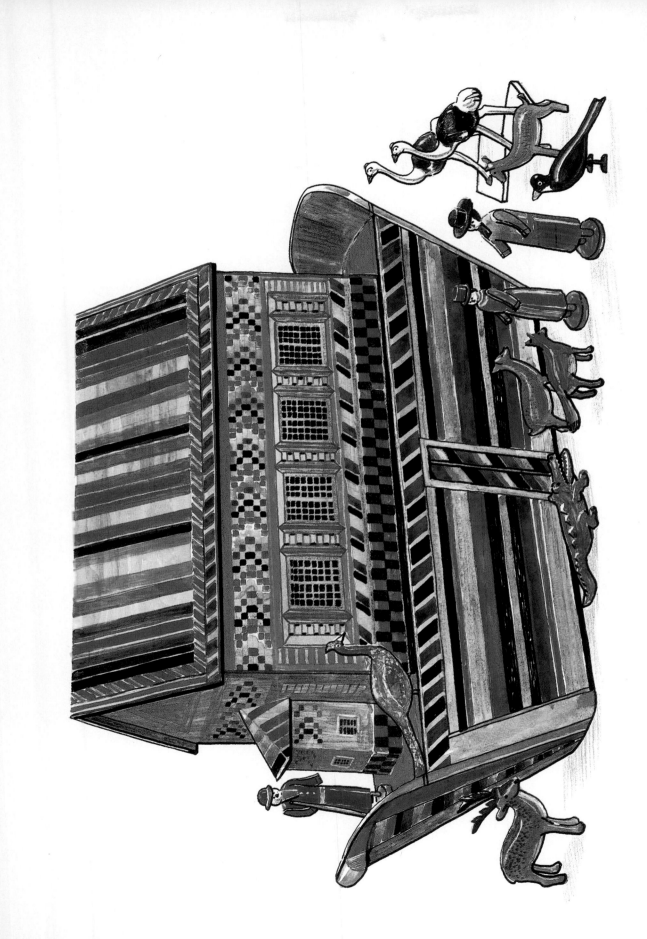

Illus. 3.   The Erzgebirge Ark (pages 85–122)

C

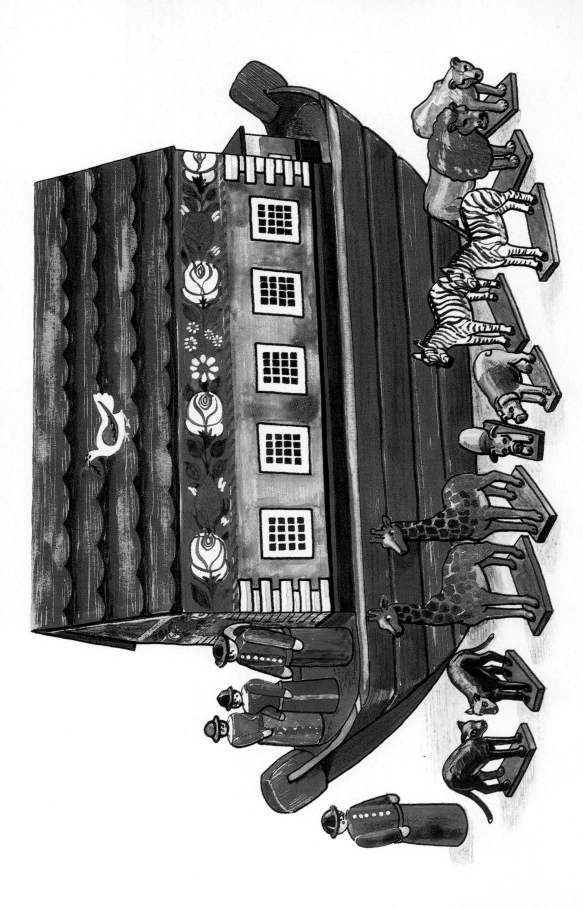

Illus. 4. The Cremer Ark (pages 123–157)

D

Project 3
Making a Polar Bear in the Pennsylvanian Tradition

Design, Structure, and Technique Considerations

A soft, cuddly, friendly, fun-loving beast? Not on your life! In fact, the polar bear is perhaps the most dangerous of all the wild animals. Weighing as much as three-quarters of a ton, the polar bear is a moody, unfriendly, awesomely powerful beast—not at all the sort of animal that you would want to cuddle. But, of course, our bear—the bear of legend and folk myth—is as wise as he is powerful and as friendly as he is strong.

As to whether or not there were white bears in the Ark, who can say? Certainly, we know that the

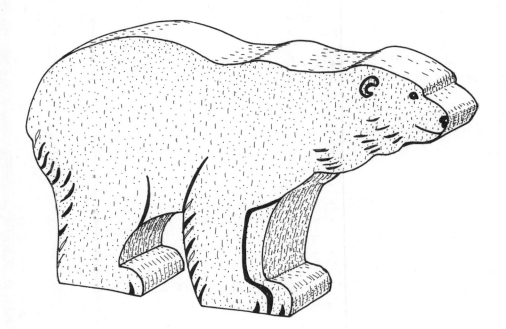

Illus. 31. Project picture. Worked in superior-quality ³/₄"-thick plywood, the polar bear measures about 4" from nose to tail. Note how, because the form is so basic, the cut edges of the ply need to be carefully worked and the "feet" edge needs to be square with the face of the ply.

33

Ark came to rest on Mount Ararat in Armenia and that it's possible to travel overland from the snowy wastes of Ararat right across Russia to the North Pole. Could it be that this magnificent beast, which is capable of travelling vast distances, simply stepped off the Ark when it came to rest in Armenia and then walked back home? Whether it did or not, the Pennsylvanian Ark wouldn't be complete if we left out the white bears.

If you look over the drawings for all the animals from all four Arks, you'll see that the white bear is perhaps the easiest to make. The rounded characteristic form is simply cut from ³/₄"-thick plywood, brought to a swift sanded finish, and painted. And there's no need for whittling, lathe turning, or any complex secondary cuts. However, because the project is so basic and has such a smooth profile is all the more reason why it needs to be crisply worked. The design must be simple yet well-considered, the various cut edges need to be carefully sawn and rubbed down so that they are at right angles to the profile face, the base has to be worked so that the animal stands upright, and the painted imagery needs to be uncomplicated and direct.

In Illus. 31, note how the plywood shape is picture-painted so that the polar bear can only be viewed correctly if seen flat-face- or side-face-on. One eye, one ear, the curve of the mouth, and the legs are seen in profile, whereas all the edge views are left plain. See how, in Illus. 33, at a scale of four grid squares to 1", the bear is about 4" from nose to tail, 2 ¹/₄" high, and ³/₄" thick.

When you have a clear understanding of the best way to work the project, visit a toy museum and look at a range of Ark animals (Illus. 32). Then sit down with a pad of work-out paper, a measure, and a pencil, and draw the bear to size and establish a crisp workable profile.

Tools and Materials

For this project you need:
- a piece of good-quality thin-veneer ³/₄"-thick multi-ply, at about 4" X 3";
- a coping saw—you might also consider a piercing saw or a fretsaw;
- a pack of graded sandpapers;

Illus. 32. Inspirational drawing. If you are looking for ideas, then it's best to go for forms that are chunky and tight. Top: North American wolverine. Left: North American Kodiak Island grizzly bear. Second top: beaver. Second bottom: North American striped skunk. Bottom: European badger.

- a V-board or a V-shaped table;
- a G-clamp;
- a sharp, small-width chisel;
- a scalpel;
- four, or more, ball-top dressmaking pins;
- primer;
- undercoat;
- varnish;
- acrylic paints;
- a selection of brushes;
- tracing paper;
- masking tape;

On the opposite page: Illus. 33. Working drawing. The scale is four grid squares to 1".

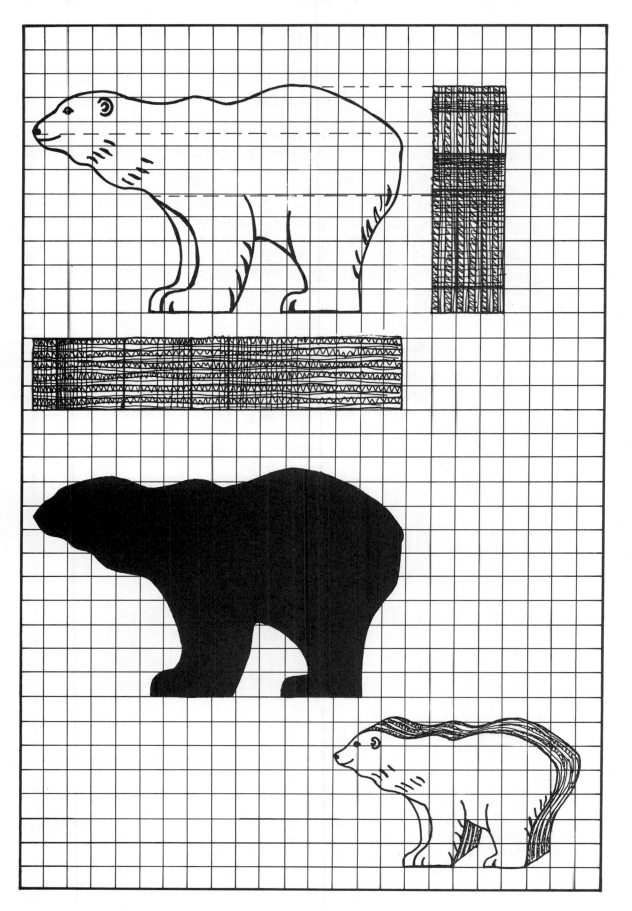

- work-out paper; and
- other workshop items, such as newspaper and paint containers.

Establishing the Design

First, set your plywood out on the workbench and look it over for possible problems. Ideally, it should be smooth, veneer-layered, white-faced, and free from splits, warps, stains, and edge cavities.

Then use a soft pencil and take a careful tracing from your master design. Place the tracing face down on the plywood, hold it secure with three or four tabs of masking tape, and then use a hard pencil to press-transfer the traced lines through to the working face of the wood (Illus. 34). When this is done, remove the tracing paper and carefully pencil in the transferred lines so that the image is clean edged. It's best to use either a hard pencil or a ball-point pen and to establish a single clear line. Next, shade in the waste, meaning all the small areas around the form that need to be cut away. Then pin up your designs and tracings so that they are in view yet out of harm's way.

Cutting the Ply

When you have press-transferred the traced image through to one of the working faces of the plywood,

position the plywood over the V-board and begin to work with your chosen saw.

Making sure that the blade is well tensioned in the saw frame, work with a steady easy action. Bearing in mind that you can either have the teeth of the saw set so that they are pointing towards the handle—in which case, you will be cutting on the pull stroke—or pointed away from the handle—in which case, you will be cutting on the push stroke—gradually saw around the form. Working at a steady pace, cut and maneuver both the blade and the wood so that the saw is always presented with the line of next cut (Illus. 35). As you are sawing, be very careful not to rip or tear the working face of the ply. When you come to sawing a tight curve, try, as you are maneuvering the wood and guiding the blade around the drawn line, to slightly increase the cutting speed so that you are, as it were, sawing on the spot.

Rubbing Down, Painting, and Finishing

Take the little sawn shape, position a sheet of coarse-grade sandpaper face-up on the workbench, and then gently rub the bear's feet, or base, backwards and forward until it stands firm and upright (Illus. 36). Be careful not to round off the cut corners of the ply; aim for a crisp square-cut finish. When this is done, take a scalpel, a chisel, or a sharp knife,

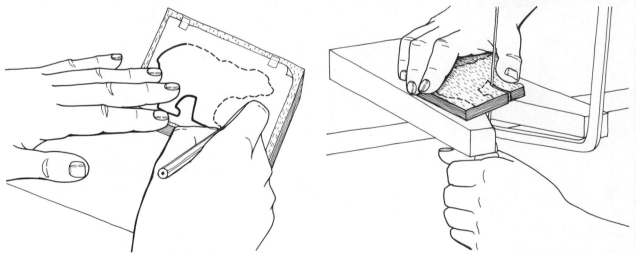

Illus. 34 (left). When you come to establishing the design, make sure that the main lines of the tracing are crisp and clean, and use a hard fine-point pencil to press the traced lines through to the working face of the wood. Illus. 35 (right). Cut and maneuver both the saw and the wood so that the blade is always presented with the line of the next cut.

36

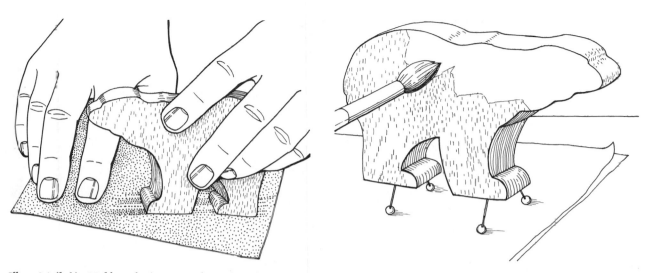

Illus. 36 (left). Holding the bear upright, rub its feet backwards and forward across the sandpaper. Continue sanding this way until the bear is able to stand firmly on its feet. Illus. 37 (right). Prior to painting, cover the work surface with newspaper, and then lift the bear well clear of the newspaper by sticking four dressmaking pins in its feet.

and work around the form, cutting in the fine corners, angles, and curves. Trim off all the little whiskers and burrs, and then go over the piece with sandpaper. Working through the graded coarse-to-smooth papers, gradually bring the sawn edges to a smooth-to-the-touch finish.

Next, take a damp cloth and wipe down the working area and the bear, making sure to clean up all the wood dust. Then stick the four ball-top dressmaker pins in the bear's feet, and see that the bear stands firm and well clear of the work surface (Illus. 37).

Once you have organized your work area and set out all your tools and paints so that they are within easy reach, start the painting process by applying a white primer. Try to work the primer into all the edges and corners. Then put the bear to one side to dry out. When the primer is dry, trim back any blobs of hard paint with the scalpel, give all surfaces a very swift rub down with the finest sandpaper, and then apply the undercoat and the gloss-white top coat. When the top coat is dry, take a little bit of black paint and your finest brush and highlight the details of the bear's eyes, ears, nose, mouth, toes, and fur

texture. Finally, apply a coat, or two, of varnish so that the piece will have a bright, white milky shine finish.

Troubleshooting and Possible Modifications

• It is most important with a project such as this that you use the best quality multilayered white-faced plywood. Be warned, if you use so-called stout-heart or soft-heart plywood—meaning plywood that has a thick, coarse, spongy center—you will undoubtedly have problems. Note: A ¾"-thick sheet of multi-ply should be made up of about 12 to 15 thin layers, or veneers.

• When choosing and using a saw, make sure that the blade is fine, sharp, and well tensioned in its frame. Before you start out on the project, you should have plenty of spare blades.

• If, after you have rubbed down the sawn edges, there still are cavities or rough edges, use a car-body filler to remedy the problem.

Project 4
Making a Bison in the Pennsylvanian Tradition

Design, Structure, and Technique Considerations

The bison is also known as the American buffalo. The tragedy is that, in 1850, there were about 60 million buffalo, but by the turn of the century, there were only a few hundred left. Shame on you, Buffalo Bill Cody and all the other hunters and so-called sportsmen who massacred the bison just for the fun of it! However, the good news is that the bison has been saved from the brink of extinction and their numbers are now steadily increasing.

As to whether or not the American bison was on Noah's passenger list, it probably wasn't, but that's

Illus. 38. Project picture. The bison, or buffalo, measures about 3" from nose to tail and 2½" from hoof to hump. Note how, if the bison is to stand firmly upright, there need to be, in profile view, two back legs and a single thickened front leg.

still no reason why we shouldn't include this noble animal.

Look at Illus. 38 and 39 and see how the American bison has certain characteristics that set him apart from his more ordinary, domesticated oxlike cousins. For example, he has massive shoulders, a pronounced hump, a huge lowering head that can't be raised to shoulder level, a thick cape of coarse fur that covers his head and shoulders, and a pair of fearsome curved horns.

Run your eyes over the working drawing (Illus. 40). See how at four grid squares to 1", and using ³/₄"-thick plywood, our bison measures about 3" long from nose to tail and 2 ¹/₂" high from hoof to hump. Referring back to Illus. 38, note how his shape is picture-painted on both flat faces of the ply. Although our bison is certainly three-dimensional, it looks like a flat two-dimensional picture when one or the other profile is viewed straight-on.

Study all the accompanying drawings; visit toy museums, zoos, and wildlife parks; collect magazine pictures; make sketches; and generally familiarize yourself with the bison. Finally, when you have decided exactly how you want your bison to look, take your paper and pencil, and draw a workable profile.

Tools and Materials

For this project you need:
- a piece of ³/₄"-thick superior-quality multi-ply, at about 3 ¹/₂" X 3";
- a coping saw, fretsaw, or piercing saw;
- a pack of blades to fit your chosen saw;
- a workbench and vise;
- a pencil, ruler, and work-out pad;
- tracing paper;
- masking tape;
- a pack of graded sandpapers;
- a selection of sanding sticks—that is, various pieces of shaped wood that can be used to support the sandpapers;
- a selection of acrylic paints;
- broad and fine-point brushes;
- a small amount of clean sand or sawdust;
- varnish; and
- workshop items, such as newspaper and mixing containers.

Illus. 39. Inspirational drawing. When you are working this type of animal it's helpful to make sketches of ideas and details. Top: Indian Mysore bull. Middle: African Cape buffalo. Bottom: East European yak.

Transferring the Design

When you have created a workable profile, go over the pencil-drawn form with a pen and make a clean crisp line. Don't worry too much at this stage about the details of the image; just try to establish the profile cutting line.

When this is done, use a soft pencil to take a tracing, turn the tracing face-down on the plywood so that the pencil line is in direct contact with the wood, and then, when you have secured the tracing with a few tabs of masking tape, press-transfer the

On the following page: Illus. 40. Working drawing. The scale is four grid squares to 1".

39

traced lines with a hard pencil through to the wood. This is perhaps a fussy and complicated process, but it does result in a good, clear, crisp transferred image. Finally, pencil over the transferred lines and shade in all the areas that need to be cut away (Illus. 41).

Sawing

Set the piece of plywood securely in the jaws of the vise, making sure that the blade of the saw is well tensioned. Starting at the back of the bison and working at a steady pace in a clockwise direction around the form, saw along the line of the back, around and over the rump, under the tail, down the back legs, under the hooves, under the belly, and so on (Illus. 42).

Holding the saw with both hands—that is, with one hand holding the handle and the other steadying and supporting the frame—keep the blade a little to the waste side of the drawn line. As you are sawing, be ready to maneuver the wood in the vise and the blade in the frame so that the saw is always presented with the line of the next cut. When you come to a tight angle—meaning a point on the profile where the cut changes direction, such as where the front legs meet the chest—you need to increase the speed of the saw while, at the same time, guiding the blade around the line. Be warned: If you

try to change the direction of the cut while the saw is at rest, you will undoubtedly break the saw blade. Also, when you are sawing, you must make sure that you hold the blade so that it passes through the thickness of the wood at right angles to the working face. Should you fail to do this, the bison would probably end up awry or lopsided.

If you have any doubts about this sawing process, we suggest that you draw a $3/4'' \times 3/4''$ square on a piece of scrap $3/4''$-thick ply and make a trial cut. If you end up with a form that is any more or less than a $3/4''$ cube, then you need more practice.

Sanding, Painting, and Finishing

Once you have fretted out the form, clear away the clutter and then prepare for the pleasurable task of rubbing the wood down to a good finish. Bearing in mind that sanding is a messy business and one that is best managed well away from your painting area, set out the graded sandpapers and your sanding sticks. For sanding sticks, you can use anything from half of an old clothespin to a piece of a wooden ruler.

Wrap the sandpaper around the sanding sticks, and begin to rub away (Illus. 43). Work the papers in a coarse-to-smooth order, over and around the form until you have achieved a super-fine, butter-smooth finish. When you come to sanding the bison's hooves, place a sheet of sandpaper face up on

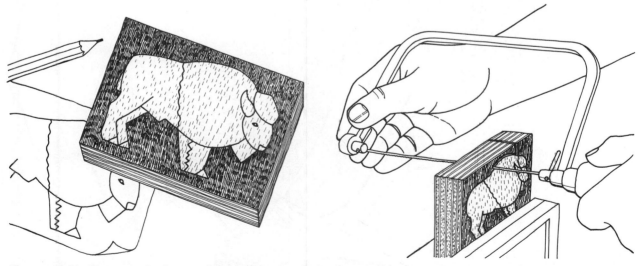

Illus. 41 (left). Press-transfer the traced image through to the working face of the wood, and shade in the areas that need to be cut away and wasted. Illus. 42 (right). Secure the plywood in the vise, make sure that the saw blade is well tensioned, and work in a clockwise direction around the form.

41

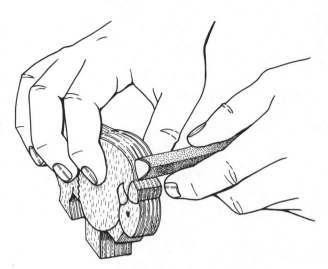

Illus. 43. Wrap the sandpaper around a suitably shaped stick, and then work the various undulations and angles of the sawn edges until they are crisp and smooth.

the bench, and then rub the sawn edge of the ply until it is smooth and at right angles to the profile's face. When the bison is able to stand firmly on its own feet, wipe it over with a damp cloth.

Make sure that the painting area is free from dust, and then set out your painting materials. Remembering to let the paint dry out thoroughly between coats, apply a primer, an undercoat, and a medium-brown top coat. When this is done, use dark-brown to paint the heavy fur cape, and white for the horns.

Then use a fine-point brush and black paint for the details on the eyes, nose, and hooves. When the paint is dry, apply a coat of varnish to the workpiece. Finally, pour a little varnish into a tub, and add enough clean sand or sawdust to make a thick gritty mixture; then paint the fur cape with this mixture to create a rugged texture (Illus. 44).

Troubleshooting and Possible Modifications

• If you decide to fill in the sawn edges prior to sanding and painting, don't use a chalky plaster-based filler; it's much better to use a two-tube resin car-body filler, instead.

• If you enjoy working with thin plywood sections, then you might modify the project and use, say, 1/4"-thick plywood and mount the animal on a base, or you might work two or three identical cutouts and use glue to build up a thicker sandwich section.

• If you like the idea of texturing the animals, then you might search out interesting materials and have, for instance, the bear trimmed with white fur, the monkey glued and dipped in flock, and so on. There are any number of exciting possibilities.

• If you decide to use a resin/hardener filler, fill the cavity so that it's slightly overfull, leave it for a short while, and then rub it back to a smooth finish.

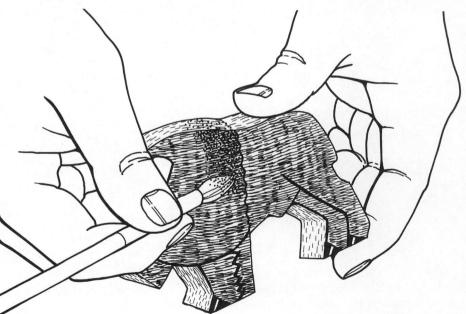

Illus. 44. Paint the bison's cape with a varnish-and-sand mixture to create a rugged-fur effect.

Project 5
Making a Monkey in the Pennsylvanian Tradition

Design, Structure, and Technique Considerations

Most of us regard monkeys as friendly, playful, fun-loving animals. Could it be that we see something of ourselves in their big-eyed, babylike faces and in their all-too-human behavior? According to Charles Darwin, monkeys and humans share the same roots. This is certainly a most thought-provoking theory, but not one that would find much favor with Mr. and Mrs. Noah! As to whether or not there were monkeys on the Ark, it's not likely that Mr. Noah, perhaps the world's first zoologist, would have sailed off without them. Baboons, woolly monkeys, chimpanzees, squirrel monkeys—the Ark was probably full of them.

Take a good look at Illus. 45 and 46 and see how our chosen chimp does, in fact, resemble a common South American woolly monkey. Then study Illus. 47 and consider how this project is similar to previous projects in that the image is flat and like a picture rather than being three-dimensional and sculptural, but its fretwork is further developed since the plywood profile is pierced.

Finally, when you have studied the remaining drawings and the suggested techniques, searched out possible alternative imagery, considered making design and technique modifications, and generally

Illus. 45. Project picture. At a scale of about four grid squares to 1", the monkey is about 2¹/₂" high.

thought through all the tool and material implications of the project, take a pad of paper and a pencil, and draw a workable profile.

Tools and Materials

For this project you need:
- a piece of ³/₄"-thick plywood, at about 2 ¹/₂" X 3";
- a coping saw;
- a pack of spare saw blades;
- a small straight saw (perhaps a tenon or a gents);
- a hand drill;
- a ¹/₈"-diameter drill bit;
- a workbench and vise;
- a pencil, ruler, and work-out pad;
- tracing paper;
- masking tape;
- a pack of graded sandpapers;
- a selection of sanding sticks;
- acrylic paints;
- brushes;
- a small scrap of sponge;
- varnish; and
- common workshop items, such as newspaper and mixing containers.

Setting Out the Design and Making Your First Cuts

Take a soft-pencil tracing from your master design, use a few tabs of masking tape to secure it face down on the piece of ply, and then take a hard pencil and press-transfer the traced lines. When this is done, remove the tracing and establish the transferred lines by going over them with a pencil.

Now, with the ply held securely in the vise, use the straight saw to cut directly in from the sides of the wood and into the various sharp peaks and angles of the profile. Working around the form in a clockwise direction, make cuts into the angle where the top of the tail meets the back, to the tip of the tail, into the foot-leg angle, into the knee-elbow angle, to the knuckles, into the crook of the elbow, and so on. Then, still working in a clockwise direction, take the coping saw and carefully work around the form, cutting away the waste (Illus. 48). As you work from cut to cut around the profile, allow the

Illus. 46. Inspirational drawing. Put together a collection of monkey and ape illustrations; there are plenty to choose from. Top left: South American marmoset. Top right: West African chimpanzee. Middle left: Asian proboscis monkey. Middle right: South American woolly monkey. Bottom left: African hamadryas baboon. Bottom right: African gorilla.

various wedges of waste to fall away. It's all relatively straightforward; you won't have any problems as long as you keep the blade moving at an even pace, be ready to reposition the wood in the vise so as to approach the line of cut to best advantage, reduce wood vibration by making sure that the line of cut is as near as possible to the vise jaws, and position the saw so that you work just a fraction of an inch on the waste side of the drawn line.

On the opposite page: Illus. 47. Working drawing. The scale is four grid squares to 1". Note the stable base, the piercing between the tail and the back, and the flat-picture imagery.

44

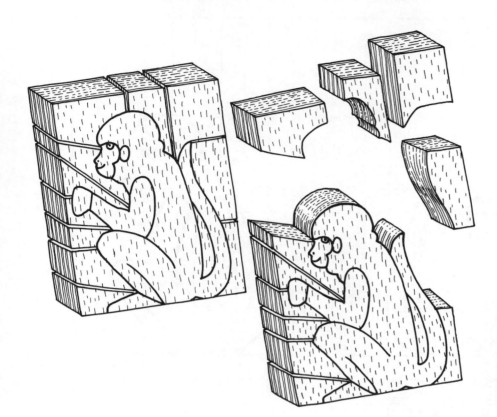

Illus. 48. Left: Once you have transferred the design, work around the profile, making straight saw cuts into the major angles and peaks. Right: Take the coping saw and cut around the profile, working from cut to cut.

Piercing

When you have cut out the profile, back it with a scrap of plywood, and then reposition it in the vise so that the area between the monkey's back and tail is uppermost (Illus. 49).

Now, set the 1/8"-diameter bit in the drill and pierce the sliver between the back and tail twice, once at the top and once at the bottom. When this is done, remove the piece of backing scrap and check to make sure that you haven't torn the surface of the ply.

If all is well, reposition the monkey and prepare to work with the coping saw; that is, unhitch the saw blade from its frame, pass it through one or the other of the drilled holes, check that the teeth are pointing away from the handle, and set it back on its pins. When you have adjusted the blade tension, carefully guide the saw blade in a clockwise direction from one hole, down the line of cut, through the other hole, and then back to the starting point. Work at a steady, even pace, making sure that the blade passes through the wood at right angles to the

working face and being careful not to twist or stress the blade while the saw is at rest. Finally, when you have cut right around the waste, ease the saw away from the monkey and remove the saw blade (Illus. 50).

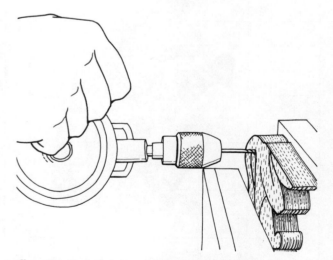

Illus. 49. Back the cutout with a piece of scrap and then drill two pilot, or guide, holes—one at the top and one at the bottom of the between-the-tail area.

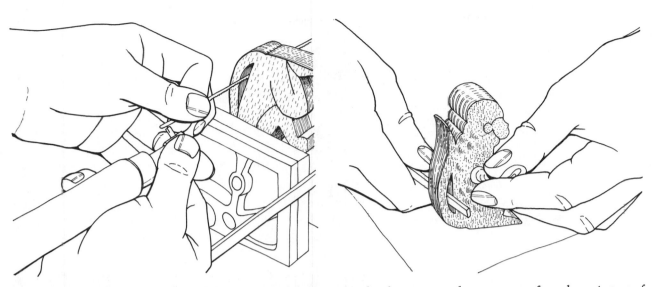

Illus. 50 (left). When you have cut all the way around the area of enclosed waste, ease the waste away from the main part of the workpiece and remove the saw blade. Illus. 51 (right). Wait a while for the top glaze to get tacky. Then take a scrap of sponge and break through the glaze with a dabbing-and-twisting action. Try to create an overall dappled or scuffed texture.

Sanding, Painting, and Finishing

Clear away all the clutter. (It's best to set up your sanding area well away from your painting area.) Then start sanding and rubbing down. Being prepared to change sanding sticks to suit the task at hand, take a medium-rough sandpaper, support it with your chosen stick, and proceed with the rubbing down. There is no single correct order or way of working. You might start with the edges and finish up with the profile faces, or you might dampen the wood slightly so as to raise the grain. It doesn't matter how you do it, as long as your workpiece comes out looking smooth and crisply worked.

When you have taken the wood to a good finish, wipe the workpiece over with a damp cloth, set up a little string drying line, and arrange all your painting materials. Remembering to let the paints dry out between coats, apply a primer, an undercoat, and a light yellow-brown glaze coat. Work the paint well into the edges and angles, check to be sure that the piece is free from any gaps and drips, and then put it to one side to dry out. When the yellow-brown glaze coat is dry, apply a darker brown top coat over it. After a short time, when the top coat is tacky, take the scrap of sponge and dab and twist it on the top glaze, revealing some of the glaze underneath and creating a dappled yellow-brown furlike texture (Illus. 51). Don't panic if the texture doesn't come out the way you want it; simply wipe the top coat off with a damp rag and try again.

Once you have achieved a good furlike texture, take a fine-point brush and a little dab of brown-black paint and highlight the various details on the face and body. Finally, when the paint is completely dry, apply a couple of coats of varnish.

Troubleshooting and Possible Modifications

• If you would rather not have a pierced area between the tail and back, you could modify the project by having the tip of the tail freestanding and set away from the body.

• If you decide to work with a thinner grade of plywood you might stick, say, two sheets of ¼" ply together with double-sided tape and fret out two identical cutouts.

• If you are intrigued by painting with glazes and creating textures, don't limit yourself to sponges. Try experimenting with other materials, such as leather, newspaper, dry brushes, and bunched-up kitchen foil.

• If you apply a coat of varnish before the top coat of paint is completely dry, the paint will wrinkle and crinkle. This may be just the effect you want.

2
THE BERCHTESGADEN ARK

The Berchtesgaden Ark (Illus. 52, and Illus. 2 on page B in the color section), a type of Ark that was made throughout the nineteenth century in the small town of Berchtesgaden in southeast West Germany, is modelled after the traditional Bavarian or Swiss Tyrolean farmhouse. This Ark has all the usual features, such as the boat base, the roofed house, the hundred, or so, paired animals, and, of course, Noah and his family. However, there are also some slightly unusual aspects to this Ark; for instance, it has wheels, the prow is upswept and has a figurehead, the house has architectural details that closely resemble those of Berchtesgaden farmhouses, and the animals appear to be boldly whittled.

As to the origins of the Berchtesgaden Ark, very little is known except that the whole area has a woodworking tradition that goes back at least to the sixteenth century. For instance, we know that in 1534, or thereabouts, a certain Wolfgang Lemberger drew up a list of trade rules for Berchtesgaden woodworkers; and we know that in the early seventeenth century, woodworkers from the area began to specialize in making clogs, rakes, boxes, and toys. It is also on record that the toy makers were so poorly paid that they referred to the Ark animals that they made as misery beasts. In the seventeenth, eighteenth, and nineteenth centuries, religious and political upheavals in and around Berchtesgaden resulted in whole groups of people emigrating; and so it was that many toy makers in the area moved to Berlin, Hanover, Nurnberg, and farther afield to America. This possibly accounts for certain Ameri-

Illus. 52. The Berchtesgaden Ark measures about 24" from prow to stern, 12" in width, and 12" from the center of the wheels to the top of the roof ridge. Note the characteristic farmhouse, the figurehead, and the large deck area.

can Arks resembling Berchtesgaden Arks and for there being doubts as to exactly where various Arks were made. Anyway, by the nineteenth century, the toy-making trade was firmly established, with all manner of Berchtesgaden wares—meaning toys, dolls, and Arks—being exported via Vienna, Antwerp, Sonneberg, and Leipzig to England, America, and the Orient.

Although, after the First World War, there was a decline in the toy-making industry, in about 1950 a group of Berchtesgaden woodworkers revived all the old toy-making traditions. They set up a "school" of woodworking that is now as busy as ever carving figures, Alpine scenes, butter and cake moulds, and nutcrackers, and making all the traditional toys—such as coaches, whistles, carts, rattles, and Noah's Arks.

Project 1
Making an Ark in the Berchtesgaden Tradition

Working Out Your Structure and Design

Before you rush out and buy all the materials for this project, stop and consider how you want your Ark to look. For example, are you going to copy the structure and design in every detail and make an exact replica? Or are you going to stay within the overall structure and design, and simply modify the specifications by using, say, a smaller scale and nontraditional materials? Consider all the tool, material, and cost implications of the project and then plan it out accordingly. If possible, visit a toy museum and take a look at early nineteenth-century German, Austrian, and Swiss Arks. It's also a good idea to make sketches, take photographs, and collect magazine clips and museum handouts.

Now, take a look at the gridded working drawings (Illus. 53 and 54) and see how, at a scale of one grid square to 2", the Ark measures 24" from prow to stern, 12" across the beam, or from side to side, and 12" from the wheel-axle center to the top of the roof ridge. Refer back to Illus. 52 and note how the overall Ark appears to be structurally complex, but is, in fact, made up of four relatively simple boxed forms: the boat-shaped base, the ground floor, the upper floor, and the roof.

Take another look at Illus. 53 and see how the design allows you to add your own modifications as the work progresses. For example, although we suggest that you use good-quality, superior-face, multicore plywood, along with small beadings, hardwood off cuts, and the like, you can alter the design and work the whole project up from, say, 1/2" X 1/2" quadrant, 1/4" X 1/4"-squared material, and thin board sections. Even though the design calls for a split roof with one half fixed and the other half hinged, there's no reason why your Ark shouldn't have a door in the side of the hull, a trapdoor in the main deck, or a lift-off house. If you want your Ark to have a larger door, more windows, a ramp, or whatever, the flexible Berchtesgaden design allows you to build in such features as you go along.

On the following pages: Illus. 53. Cutting grid. The scale is about one grid square to 1". Illus. 54. The working drawing. Top: The scale is one grid square to 1". Middle and bottom: section and details, not to scale. Note the interior beadings, the slotted half-lap attachment of the house walls, and the axle fittings.

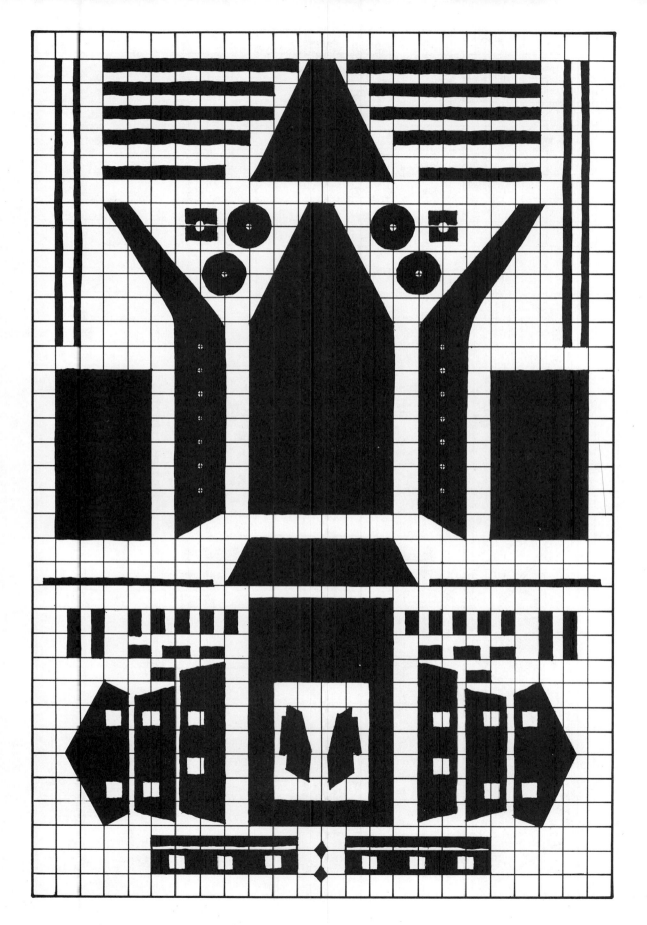

51

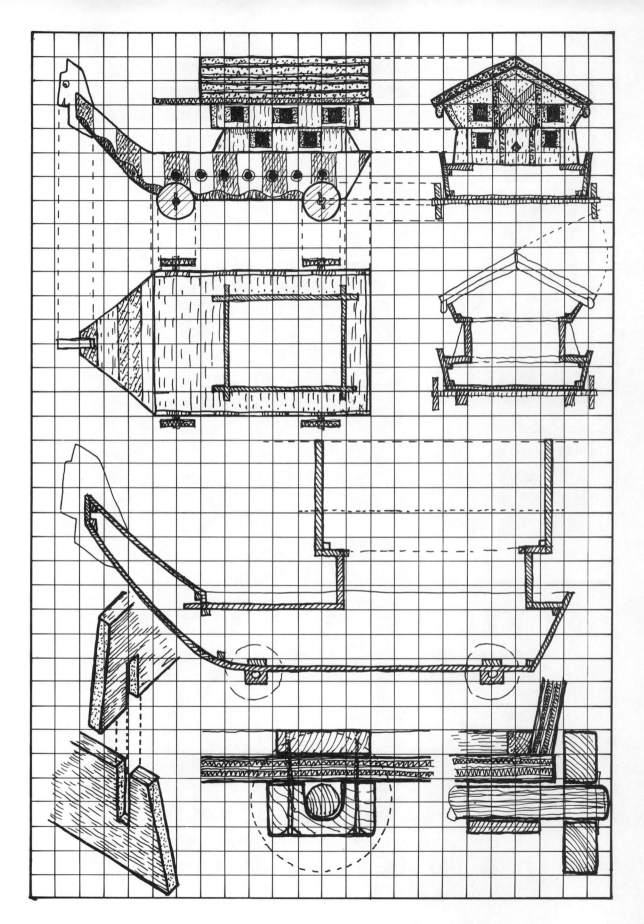

Tools and Materials

For this project you need:
- about 16 square feet of ³⁄₈"-thick, good-quality, superior-face multicore plywood;
- about 30 feet of ¹⁄₂" X ¹⁄₂" beading (you can use plywood offcuts);
- about 36" of ³⁄₈"-diameter dowelling;
- a good selection of workshop offcuts;
- plastic wood filler, or stopper;
- a good selection of superior-quality, enamel, high-gloss model-makers' paints (preferably primary colors);
- a can of white primer;
- a can of white undercoat;
- a can of yacht varnish;
- a selection of both fine-point and broad brushes;
- a small straight saw—either a tenon or a gents;
- a small nail hammer;
- a measure and a metal straightedge;
- a coping saw with a pack of spare blades;
- a hand drill and a selection of drill bits;
- a set square;
- white PVA wood glue;
- a quantity of small brass brads;
- three small brass hinges with brass countersunk screws to fit;
- a small flat rasp of the Surform type;
- a round-section Surform tube rasp;
- a pack of graded sandpapers;
- a compass;
- pencils and work-out paper;
- a sharp fine-point knife;
- a heavy craft knife; and
- a workbench and vise.

The Hull, Main Deck, and Prow Deck

Look at Illus. 55 and see how the hull has a single-board flat bottom that runs from the stern and curves up towards the prow, side-beam boards that angle up and in towards the prow, a main deck, and a flat prow deck. Then in Illus. 56 note how the house sits squarely over a pierced deck hatch.

Now, with a pencil, measure, and straightedge, set the two identical profiles of the boat sides and the stern board out on the plywood, mark out and check

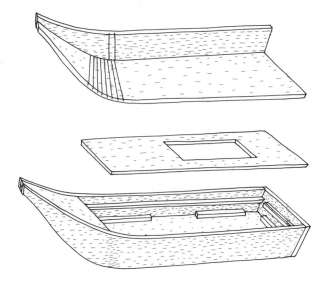

Illus. 55. Top: Secure one of the side boards; then carefully ease the kerf-cut base and side boards together until the mating edges are aligned. Middle and bottom: Locate the main deck on the beading.

the angles at the prow and stern, and then use a straight saw to cut out the forms. If you refer back to Illus. 55, you will see that although the side-beam boards angle sharply in towards the prow, the Ark's base board travels up in a smooth curve. So, once you have cut and shaped the two side boards, place them on the base board and mark off the 2–3" run that needs to be curved.

Now, take the straight saw and work a series of saw kerfs across the base board on what will be the

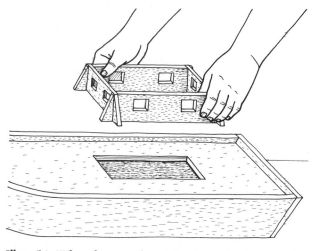

Illus. 56. When the main deck is in place, slot the ground-floor walls together, check to make sure that the resultant box shape fits over the hatchway, lift the deck, and then fit and attach the walls.

inside of the curve. Space the kerfs about $\frac{1}{4}$" apart and stop short when you have cut about three-quarters of the way through the thickness of the wood. Continue cutting kerfs across the width and through the thickness of the base board until you can ease and bend it up so that it follows the prow profile.

Now, secure one of the side boards in the vise so that its bottom edge is uppermost, and then use PVA glue and a handful of brass brads to fit and attach the base. Work from the stern and nail the base to the side at 1" intervals. When you have nailed and glued both sides, place the hull frame on the work surface and gently ease the sides out to a slight angle. Now, take the stern board and adjust its shape until it sits flush on the base board and holds the side boards out at the correct angle. When you have cut and rubbed down the stern board so that it has a good fit, attach it with brass brads and PVA glue, as already described.

When you have achieved a fairly well shaped hull, use either thin strips taken from off cuts or lengths of $\frac{1}{2}$" x $\frac{1}{2}$" beading to strengthen all the inside angles. Simply take the beading, cut it to the required lengths, use a Surform and sandpaper to shape them to suitable sections, bed them in glue, and then butt them into all the interior side-to-base angles. When the glue is dry, measure up from the base board and mark off the deck level. If your Ark has 4"-high sides, the main deck needs to be placed about 3" up from the base. Run the deck line right around the inside of the hull (that is, around the two sides and the stern), and then glue and nail lengths of $\frac{1}{2}$" x $\frac{1}{2}$" beading on the line to provide a lip, or ledge support, for the deck board.

When you come to fitting the deck, first aim for a good side and stern fit, and then cut it to length so that its leading edge occurs just under the aft line of the prow deck. Once you have worked the main deck to a good fit, secure it in the vise and use a coping saw to cut out the 8" x 10" hatchway. Finally, dribble glue on the ledge support and drop the main deck in position.

Fit the prow deck in the same manner, but place the support beading so that the deck surface rises at an angle and is lined up level and flush with the top edge of the prow board. When you have shaped, fitted, and glued the prow deck in position, cut a small riser strip to bridge the gap between the main deck and the prow deck and then attach it with glue and brads.

Finally, stop up all gaps and raw edges with a little filler and then use graded sandpapers to rub the wood down to a good, silky smooth, with-the-grain finish.

The Ground Floor of the Farmhouse

Take the 4"-wide wall strips—which you can get directly from 4"-wide board or work from plywood—and mark, measure, and cut them to size. Now, look at Illus. 56 and see how the boards cross over at the corners and are slotted so that they can be interlocked.

It's best to work the corner joints, simply notched half-laps, with a straight saw and a coping saw. First, make sure that all four boards have their end angles going in the correct direction; then take a pencil and clearly label them *top edge* and *outside face*. One piece at a time, set the wood in the vise and use a measure, square, and pencil to mark in the position of the eight half-lap notches. Now, use the straight saw to work the two parallel cuts, which should be slightly more than 2" long and set apart the thickness of the wood. Use the coping saw to link the bottom of the cuts, and try to finish the half-lap notches so that the boards slot together to make a tight fit. If necessary, use a file or a knife and a scrap of sandpaper to rub the wood down to size.

When the four strips have been cut and notched to a good a fit, establish how the box shape should be placed over the main deck hatch and then label one of the two short sides *front with door* and the other *stern*.

With a pencil and ruler, set out the position of the front door, the door posts, the little diamond-shaped detail in the middle of the door, the window holes, and the window shutters. Now, a length at a time, set the wood in the vise and pierce each window position with a saw-blade pilot hole; that is, use the hand drill and a $\frac{1}{4}$" drill bit to work a starter hole in each of the window positions. When this is done, unhitch the coping saw blade, pass it through the pilot hole, retension the blade in its frame, and then begin to saw. Work at a steady pace and try, as you are sawing, to hold the frame so that the blade is at right angles to the working face of the wood. Continue in this manner until you have cut out all eight windows. As for all the little details, meaning the window shutters and the door trim, it's best to work them from veneer scraps or off cuts and then attach them with glue.

The Upper Floor

Take a look at Illus. 52 and 57 and see how the two shaped end gables are linked by two side strips and how the shape of the gable sets the angle, or pitch, of the roof.

First, cut the two identical gable forms, making sure that each is symmetrical, and then take a pencil and label them so that the best, or working, faces look outward. Now, take the two long side strips, having first cut out the window holes with the drill and the coping saw, and create the boxed form using the glue, brads, and beading.

If you place the upper floor on the lower floor, you will see that, although it is well supported by the notched, or slotted, corners, the underside of the overhang, or jetty, needs to be boxed in on all four sides with little fillet strips. This being so, flip the upper floor over, cut the strips slightly wider than the overhang, and then glue and nail them in place so that the extra width faces towards the inside of the house.

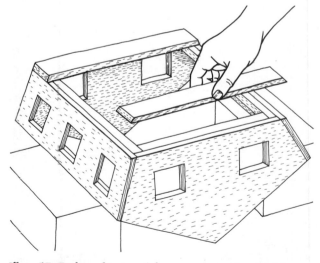

Illus. 57. Reduce the size of the upper storey by attaching strips of wood to the underside edge. Note how the partially built box is being supported and cradled on a couple of blocks.

Now, place the upper floor on the lower, making sure that it is positioned squarely and that the gable ends are facing towards the prow and the stern, and then attach it with glue and brads. Wait for the glue to dry; then strengthen all inside angles with off cuts bedded in glue.

Some Arks like this are built so that the upper floor lifts off. If you want to build this feature into your design, don't glue and nail the upper floor to the lower, but rather position it on location dowels or use hinges.

When you have finished the basic box structure, use veneer strips or thin pieces of off cuts to make the various decorative details, the window shutters, the corner boards, the vertical members, and the crossed gable braces. Finally, strengthen all inside angles with off cuts bedded in glue, trim the top edge of the wall and gable with 1/2" X 1/2" beading, and rub down all cut edges to a good smooth finish.

The Roof

Look at Illus. 58 and see how the roof is made up from two main boards and various pieces of gable and gutter trim. The way you fit the roof to the gable is a design feature that requires some consideration. For example, would you like to be able to lift the roof off as a single fixed unit? Do you want the two sides of the roof to be hinged at the gutter so that they split at the ridge and open outward and downwards? Or do you want to follow the project closely and have one half of the roof fixed and the other half hinged at the ridge line? Whichever alternative you choose, you will first need to measure the upper story of the house from gutter to ridge line and from gable to gable, and then use the straight saw and the rasp to cut out the two main roof boards, allowing for a generous gable and gutter overhang.

Making sure that the wood is square, fit, glue, and nail one half of the roof directly to the wall and gable. When this is done, edge the fitted half of the roof at the gutter and ridge with a length of decorative beading. Edge the other half of the roof in a similar manner, wait for the glue to dry, and then use the three small brass hinges to link the two roof halves at the ridge line.

When you reach this stage, take a breather from your work and review the accompanying drawings

Illus. 58. When the house has been attached to the deck and the deck has been located and attached on its lip, or ledge, then fit and hinge the roof boards.

and any other material that you might have collected. Note how we have finished off the project by using gable boards, roof battens, and pebbles to create the effect of a traditional Bavarian farmhouse. Of course, you could, for example, leave out the pebbles and battens and use shingles instead; or you could use gable boards that are decoratively pierced and carved in the Swiss Tyrolean tradition. Give some thought to the various alternatives. Finally, cut and carve the figurehead, which you might want to personalize in some manner. Then glue and nail the figurehead into a saw-worked prow slot.

The Wheels

See how the wheels are depicted in Illus. 52, 54, and 59. The axles are free-moving but held securely by simple U-bearings that are screwed to the underside of the Ark.

Start by measuring the width of the Ark, allowing for the wheel thickness and the hub wedge brads, and then cut the two dowel axles to length. Now, take a couple of 2" X 2" X 2" off cuts, preferably from a close-grained, knot-free hardwood, and secure pairs of blocks in the vise; then use a round-section tube rasp or a tool of your choice to cut the bearings. If you are making the bearings to take a piece of ½" dowel, cut a U-shaped groove that is slightly deeper

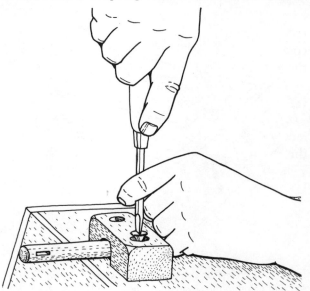

Illus. 59. Turn the Ark upwards, mark out the position of the axles, and use screws to attach the axle U-bearings.

and wider than ½". Align the two axles (that is, make sure that they are parallel with each other and square with the base), and then drill and screw the U-bearings in place.

All you need to do to make the wheels is scribe circles out on the plywood and use a coping saw and sandpaper to work four discs.

When you come to fitting the wheels, drill them to fit the axle dowel, allowing for a small amount of free play on the axle; then take a small drill bit, say, a ⅛" diameter, and drill a wedge hole through the thickness of the axle at a point between the wheel and the dowel end. Do this with all four wheels. Finally, cut four little wedge-shaped hub brads, locate them in the axle holes, and tap them home.

Painting

Once you have completed building the Ark and have rubbed down all sharp edges, rough corners, and brad points, clear your workbench of all clutter and make sure that your entire work area is free from dust and dirt. Then set out all your paints and brushes so that they are comfortably at hand.

Take a cloth dampened in turpentine and wipe the surface of the Ark. Then, rubbing down between coats, apply a couple of generous coats of white primer. Starting inside the Ark in the most inaccessible corners, work the paint into every nook and cranny, paying particular attention to end-grain edges and areas that you anticipate are going to receive the most knocks. Wait until the primer is completely dry; then repeat the procedure, but this time use the white undercoat instead.

When you come to painting the gloss top coat, first pencil in the various color blocks, and then use a medium-broad brush to paint the largest and the most awkward areas. You might use white paint for the Ark interior, green paint for the main deck, and yellow paint for the walls and roof of the farmhouse. However, the real fun starts when you begin painting all the little decorative details (Illus.60) because this gives you a chance to personalize the Ark. For

instance, you can paint a number or name on the door, flowers up the walls, and maybe a dove or two on the roof. Look over the other projects for additional ideas.

Finally, when you have finished all the decora-

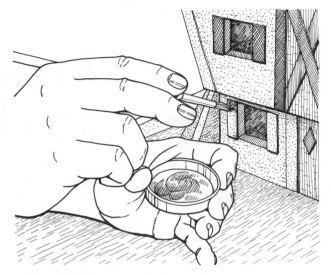

Illus. 60. When all the trim has been cut, fitted, attached, and given a coat of base color, bring out the details with a fine-point brush.

tive details and waited a day or two for the paint to dry, sign and date the bottom of the Ark, apply a generous coat of yacht varnish, and the job is done.

Troubleshooting and Possible Modifications

• It is very important to rub back all sharp edges and brad points. For the sake of safety, you might use screws rather than brads.

• Once the Ark has been assembled, it's quite difficult to paint the interior. Therefore, you might prefer to paint the Ark at the end of each stage.

• Make sure that all materials are nontoxic. Use lead-free paints, for example.

• If you anticipate keeping a hundred, or so, animals in the Ark, it's a good idea to build a trapdoor hatchway in either the prow deck or the stern.

Project 2
Whittling a Figure in the Berchtesgaden Tradition

Design, Structure, and Technique Considerations

Take a look at Illus. 61, and note how Mr. and Mrs. Noah have been made using a very basic whittling technique. Also, see how these figures have a beautifully direct and open angular quality about them. Then take a look at Illus. 62 and 63 and note that, at six grid squares to 1", the figures measure about 3½" from base to hat.

Before you begin whittling these figures, visit the nearest folk-art or a toy museum and try to see some whittled and carved dolls, skittles, and pull-along figures that were made in nineteenth-century Switzerland, Germany, Poland, and America. Make comparisons, and notice how, for example, figures made in Oberammergau have been carved to a relatively slick finish, whereas figures made in Seiffen have been turned and carved and then painted to a high finish, and those made in Sonneberg are really no more than stylized bobbin dolls. Handle as many traditional dolls and Ark figures as possible, noting their weight and size, and the way they have been carved, painted, and assembled. Generally, enjoy yourself spending some time getting to know your subject.

Finally, take a look at all of the remaining drawings for this project. You will see how, although we

Illus. 61. Project picture. The figures stand at about 3½" to 4" in height. See the crisply worked details of the hat, faces, and hands. Note that the poles and the base slabs are additions.

58

only show you how to make Mr. Noah, when you come to making the other seven figures, all you will need to do is slightly modify the forms and decorative details. For example, you can work Noah's three sons so that they are a fraction of an inch shorter and without beards, and Mrs. Noah can be about the same size as her husband but her features can be smaller and she can be wearing a head scarf and an apron. Follow the general step-by-step directions, but be ready to adjust the designs from figure to figure.

Tools and Materials

For each figure in this project you need:
- a piece of 2" X 2" lime wood that is 4" long;
- a piece of 2" X 2", ¼"-thick lime for the base of the figure;
- a couple of knives (say, one with a fine sharp-point blade and one with a broad blade);
- a coping saw with a pack of spare blades;
- a pencil and work-out paper;
- a 1-pound pack of Plasticine;
- a pack of graded sandpapers;
- a couple of small, fine-pointed riffler files;
- a selection of high-gloss model-makers' paints;
- a small can of white undercoat;
- a small can of white primer;
- a small can of yacht varnish;
- a small can or tube of plastic filler; and
- all the usual items, such as brushes, turpentine cloths, wire, newspaper, and a workbench.

Setting Out the Design and Making a Plasticine Model

First, glance over all your working drawings and the accompanying illustrations as well as any other material that you may have collected. Pay special attention to Illus. 61–63, taking note of the overall stance of the figures as well as the details of their hands, feet, and faces.

Then, working at a scale of six grid squares to 1", start to build a prototype model, or maquette, of a figure that's about 3–4" high (Illus. 64). Consider the squareness of Mr. Noah and how one of his arms is straight whereas the other is crooked; then cut and work the Plasticine accordingly. Of course, if you

want to change the pose slightly and leave out the staff or have the figure hunched or whatever, now's your chance to work out these modifications. You'll need to make a separate working model for each figure.

Marking Out the Design and Making Your First Cuts

When you have a good understanding of how the figure ought to be carved, use tracing paper and transfer the lines of the various views to the working faces of one of the 2" X 2" X 4" pieces of lime wood (Illus. 65). You can also work by eye and eliminate the use of the tracing paper. Now, bearing in mind that with this type of figure you only want to carve a simple caricature, take the coping saw and eliminate the large areas of waste. For example, with Mr. Noah, you will need to clear away the wood from underneath his crooked arm, from either side of his head, from underneath his right arm, from between the hem of his smock and his shoes, and from between his legs.

Once you have cleared the waste from both the side profile and the front view, reestablish the pencil-drawn guidelines. Now, take one of your knives and make stop cuts around the figure at all the main stepping points. There should be cuts around the top of the hat brim, on the underside of the hat between the brim and the top of the shoulders, and so on. Cut to a depth of about ⅛".

When you have cut in all the main design lines, take another look at Illus. 61–63 and establish in your mind's eye exactly how you want your figure to look, and then start whittling and carving in earnest. Work the heaviest and deepest areas first, holding the wood firmly in one hand with the head end nearest you and holding the knife as if you were going to pare an apple. Begin by chopping the area between the top line of the shoe and the hem, working the line of the legs. Don't attempt to create

On the following pages: Illus. 62 (left). Working drawing for Mr. Noah. The scale is six grid squares to 1". Note the overall square shape and the compact forms. Illus. 63 (right). Working drawing for Mrs. Noah. The scale is six grid squares to 1". Note the heavy lumps for the shoes and the way the back of the head scarf tilts up.

Illus. 64. Establish the basic shape, the forms, and the details by building a Plasticine model.

realistic-looking legs; just make shapes that suggest legs. Next, work the areas between the legs and on the underside of the smock hem, and then move on. Bear in mind that as you are working the various

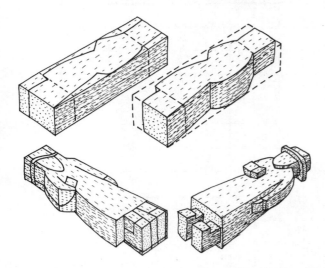

Illus. 65. Top left: Mark out the front view and shade in the areas that need to be wasted. Top right: Use the coping saw to clear away the waste. Bottom left: Mark in the various front and side details. Bottom right: Use a knife to lower the wood, aiming to achieve the main form-describing planes.

levels and planes, you will have to keep the wood moving to obtain the best angle of cut. You shouldn't have any problem as long as you keep your knife sharp and make sure that the blade is always under control, being especially careful not to let the blade run into the wood and thereby split off areas of end grain. Continue deepening the stop cuts and working at an angle into the cuts to establish the broad forms—the shoes, the smock hem, the two fists, the cuffs, the crooked elbow, the shoulders, and the hat.

Whittling the Body Details

When you have roughed out the basic forms, spend a couple of minutes clearing the work surface, sharpening your knives, and taking another look at your drawings and model. Now, go back to the little roughed-out figure and try to estimate just how much wood needs to be removed. Visualize the finished figure as if it were concealed just below the surface of the wood. With this in mind, repeat the stop-cutting procedure you used for the roughing out, only this time work on a much smaller, finer scale (Illus. 66).

For example, when you work the hands, take a

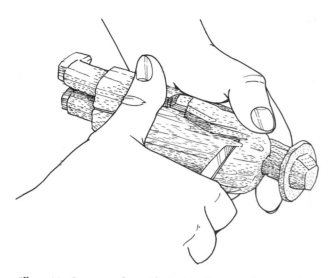

Illus. 66. *Once you have blocked in the main forms and rounded them off, then take a fine-point knife or scalpel and cut in the details.*

fine-point knife or scalpel and make little form-describing, between-finger V-cuts. You should take note of the various planes that make up the shape of the fist, and then establish the spacing of the fingers and the thumb with four cuts. When this is done, increase the depth and width of the cuts until the half-rounded finger shapes begin to emerge from the wood. Work both hands in this manner, but when you come to working the right hand, make allowances for a staff hole by either leaving an area that can be drill-pierced at a later stage or working a hole with the point of a knife.

As you whittle, always keep the knives razor-sharp and be constantly aware of the changing grain of the wood. Certainly, if you are working with a good piece of knot-free lime, your grain difficulties will be minimal, but you will still need to continually modify the angle of cut to suit the task at hand. Remember to cut in the creases that occur between the arms and the body, and to cut the folds and tucks at the shoulders and in the crook of the arm.

Modelling the Head

Study all of the pertinent drawings and any other inspirational material, and, if necessary, have another go at it with the Plasticine or perhaps with a small piece of scrap wood. Consider the face in both profile and front views and see how, as with the rest

of the figure, the features are made up of a series of stepped stop cuts.

Hold the figure in your hand or support it on a wad of rags or on a wooden V-block cradle, and cut in the edges of the hat brim, the line of the brow, the eye line, the line of the ears, and the mouth (Illus. 67). Work the face the way you worked the hands, but be extra careful that the knife doesn't slip and split off pieces of delicate short grain.

Start by cutting in the line at the top of the hat brim, and then make a series of paring cuts into the stop cut to lower the wood. When you have cleared away the rough to the depth of the first stop cut, make another stop cut and continue paring as before. Gradually work deeper and deeper into the wood this way until you have carved the little rounded hat dome. The area below the hat brim and the delicate features need to be worked in a similar manner. As you near completion of the head, work with smaller and smaller thumb-paring cuts until you have whittled out Noah's face, hat, and beard.

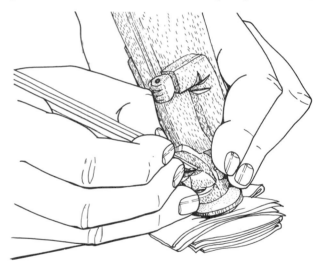

Illus. 67. *Support the head on a wad of rags. Making sure that you don't split off the short grain of the hat brim, cut in the various steps and planes that make up the face.*

Completing the Carving

When you feel you are done, clear away the clutter, set the carving up on a dais, and then stand back and be critical. Ask yourself these kinds of questions: Are his features well enough defined? Could the

Project 3
Whittling a Hippopotamus in the Berchtesgaden Tradition

Design, Structure, and Technique Considerations

The dictionary describes a hippopotamus as being a massive gregarious mammal, or a short, thick-skinned, slightly hairy, fat-legged beast. Certainly, hippos in the flesh aren't a pretty sight; but with their generous proportions, ever-open cavelike mouth, and mud-wallowing nature, Berchtesgaden Ark hippos can be absolutely charming.

Take a look at Illus. 70 and note all the characteristics that go into making up a hippo. Your hippo-

Illus. 70. Project picture. The hippo is about 3" long and 2" high. Note that the teeth are pegs, that their holes have been drilled, and that they've been attached with glue.

66

Illus. 71. Inspirational drawing. Consider making other unusual armored, long-nosed, and horned animals; there are plenty to choose from. Top: African white rhinoceros. Second from top: American armadillo. Middle: South American hairy armadillo. Second from bottom: American desert tortoise. Bottom: Malaysian tapir.

potamuses, or hippopotami (don't forget that you need to make a Mr. and a Mrs.), should be well-rounded, and should have a large open mouth ringed with plenty of peglike teeth, largish ball-like eyes, and perhaps most important of all, somewhere between their wide-open mouth and stumpy fat legs, a nicely rippled, short, fat neck.

Take a pad of work-out paper to a toy museum or, perhaps better still, a zoo, and make a series of hippo sketches. Don't worry too much about realism because, after all, it's doubtful whether any of the Berchtesgaden animal carvers had ever seen a hippo; just do your best to capture the essentials. It's also a good idea at this stage to make models in Plasticine. Also, list color and measurement details and note

how, with the hippo, the grain can run either vertically from the base to the back or horizontally from the nose to the tail.

Tools and Materials

For this project you need:
- a piece of 3" X 3" lime wood that is 4" long;
- a 3" X 4" piece of ¼"-thick lime for the base;
- a small straight saw;
- a coping saw with a pack of spare blades;
- a selection of knives, including a knife with a strong broad blade and a fine-point scalpel;
- a pencil and a pad of work-out paper;
- a pack of graded sandpapers;
- a small riffler file;
- a small hand drill with a ⅛"-diameter drill bit;
- five cans of enamel paint, in black, black-brown, pink, green, and red;
- a can of primer;
- a can of undercoat;
- a can of yacht varnish;
- a small quantity of hair, fur, or bristle;
- a selection of brushes; and
- workshop items, such as cloths, paint cleaner, and newspaper.

Transferring the Design and Making Your First Cuts

First, set your wood out on a workbench and check it over to make sure that it's free from faults. Ideally, you need a piece of wood that has a good straight grain—one that's free from cracks, splits, and knots. Now, take a tracing from your master design, and then, with a pencil, carefully press-transfer the lines of the traced design through to the various working faces of your piece of wood. At this stage, don't bother to draw in the front and rear view details; just try to establish the main side view, or profile. Label the various faces of the wood *top*, *base*, and *front*, and then shade in all the areas that need to be wasted.

Now, secure the wood in a vise so that you can see

On the following page: Illus. 72. Working drawing. The scale is about three grid squares to 1". Note that the grain of the wood needs to run from the nose to the tail.

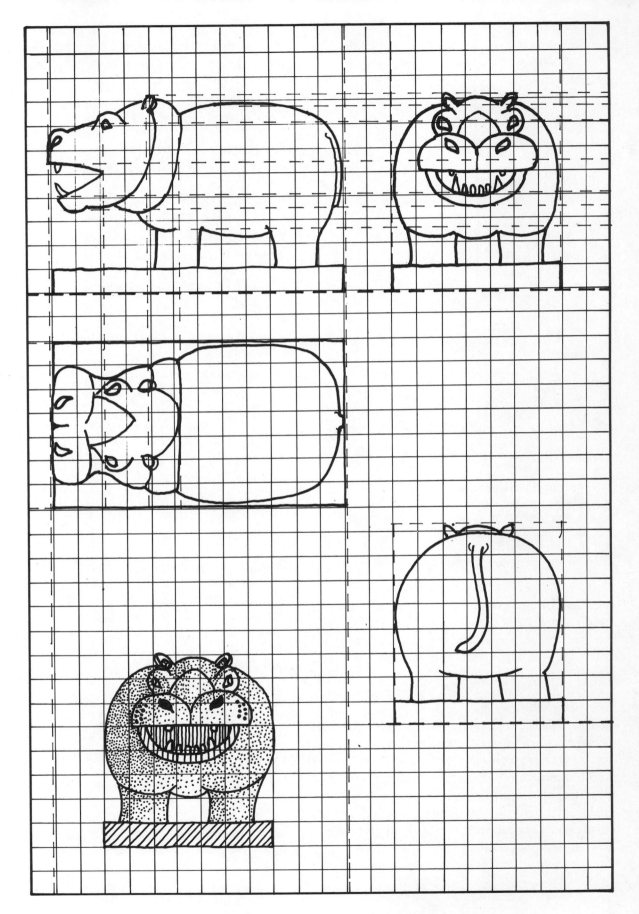

the hippo in profile and begin cutting out the main form with the coping saw. Don't try too hard to follow the outline; just try to remove the bulk of the waste (Illus. 73). When this is done, redraw any pencil lines that have become blurred, and reestablish the nose and tail ends. Finally, with the wood repositioned and held securely in the vise so that the feet are uppermost, take the small gents saw and make a single center-line cut that divides the backleg block, just touches and follows the line of the belly, and divides the front-leg block.

Roughing Out the Form

Before you go any further, make sure that your knives are razor-sharp. Probably for about every 10 minutes spent carving, you will have to spend 5 minutes with an oilstone putting new edges on your blades. Now, with the wood still secure in the vise so that the feet are uppermost, take the coping saw and make four more cuts—one on either side of the two initial cuts. Cut straight down and then curve into the bottom of the middle cut to establish the vertical faces of all four inside legs (Illus. 74). If you've done

this correctly, you should be able to lift out four little wedges—two from between the front legs and two from between the back.

When you have removed these wedges from between the legs, refer back to Illus. 70 and draw in the position of the ears, the creases and bulges underneath the lower jaw, the underbelly, and so on. Now, with the hippo cradled upside down in the palm of your hand, or, if you prefer, on a wad of rags on the bench, take a knife and start to whittle the shape of the four short legs. Keeping an eye on the run of the grain, work very gradually towards the desired form. When you are carving the belly, cutting in the fatty ripples around the neck, shaping the rump, and generally working towards a well-defined form, be sure to keep the wood moving so as to approach the grain to best advantage.

Final Modelling

When you have achieved what you consider to be a well-roughed-out hippo, stand it next to the Ark and the carved figures and see how it relates. Bear in mind that although the hippo doesn't need to be

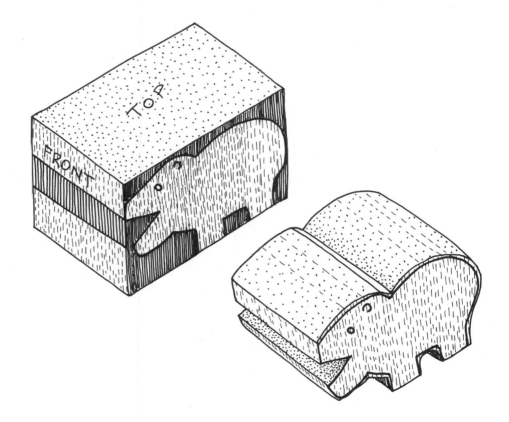

Illus. 73. Left: Establish the profile, label the faces, or views, and then shade in the areas that need to be wasted. Right: Use the saw of your choice to cut away the waste.

worked to a true scale, for best effect it should be finished and decorated in the same manner as the other pieces.

With this in mind, take a soft pencil and firmly draw in the shape of the ears and eyes, the position of the nostrils, the number and position of the teeth, and so forth. Now, take your chosen tool (we prefer using a very small, sharp-bladed penknife) and cut in these details (Illus. 75). Of course, as with the other projects, you must at all times be aware of the run and direction of the grain. The hippo is relatively easy to work because the legs are short and stubby, but it's also a bit tricky since there are areas of short grain around the open mouth. Therefore, take it easy when you come to carving the area under the jaw. You'll need to cut and shape the bulging eyes, carve the stubby ears, and repeatedly rework various areas until they meet your approval.

When you come to fitting the hippo's teeth, secure the workpiece in a well-muffled vise, making sure that the lower jaw is padded and supported, and then prepare to work with the hand drill and the smallest drill bit (Illus. 76). Now's your chance to do a bit of dentistry, but instead of drilling holes and taking teeth out, you will be drilling holes and putting teeth in. Make the holes about ⅛" deep; then sharpen little peg-shaped pieces of waste, dip them in glue, and push them into the holes.

Finally, rub the hippo's feet on a sheet of sandpaper until it can stand upright, and then glue the hippo in position on the little ¼"-thick base.

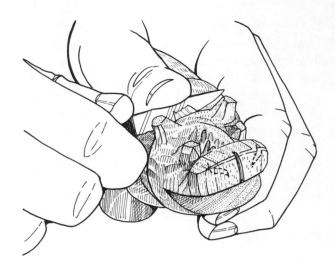

Illus. 75. Once you have sawn and blocked out the basic shape, use a knife to round off the main form and then use a small knife to work the fine details.

Finishing and Painting

When the glue is dry, go over the workpiece swiftly with sandpaper and a scalpel, and then wipe it over with a turpentine-dampened cloth. Now, consider the hippo's girth and the size of your can of paint, and decide on your best approach—either dipping the workpiece in the can of paint or painting it with a brush. We have chosen to do both. Start by dipping the workpiece in the primer and letting it dry; then trim off any paint runs and dip it in the undercoat. If you refer to the drawing of the Berchtesgaden Ark on page B in the color section, you will see that the hippo has a black-brown body, a pink-red mouth, white teeth, and a green base. With the hippo positioned on a painting dais (you can also use a revolving pottery turntable), take a broad soft-haired brush and apply the black-brown paint to the body. Start by painting all the tricky little areas under the belly, work up and over the back, and then finish up with the face. When this is done, wait until the paint is nearly dry, and then, being careful not to paint the teeth, dab in the pink-red mouth and the black eyes. When the base has been painted green and everything is dry, varnish the entire workpiece.

Finally, after an hour or two when the varnish is still tacky, take a small pinch of hair, bristle, or fur, and sprinkle it over the sticky hippo's back and

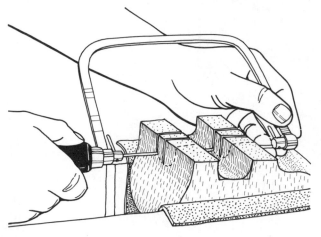

Illus. 74. With the coping saw, make four cuts—one on either side of the two initial cuts, establishing the vertical faces of all four legs.

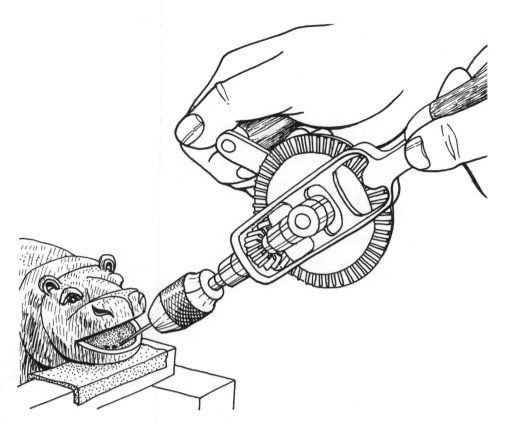

Illus. 76. Secure the hippo in the muffled vise, making sure that the bottom jaw is well supported; then drill the tooth holes.

rump, creating a sparse but rather attractive covering of hair.

Troubleshooting and Possible Modifications

• With most of the animals, the grain of the wood really should run vertically from the base to the back to give strength to the legs and to minimize weak short-grain areas. But since the hippo has such short legs, if you wish you can have the grain running horizontally from the nose to the tail.

• Always select your wood with great care, making sure that it is well-seasoned and free from knots, stains, and splits. Be warned that if you work with sappy new wood, there is a chance that as the wood dries out, the workpiece will split and break up.

• Although you might alter the working order slightly, it's best to always start by cutting away the large areas of waste from the body and finish by working the fragile face details.

Project 4
Whittling a Camel in the Berchtesgaden Tradition

Design, Structure, and Technique Considerations

The camel is a large, hornless, humpbacked, long-necked, long-legged, broad-footed, and cud-chewing mammal, which is used as a beast of burden in Africa and the East. There are two species—the Arabian camel, or dromedary, with one hump, and the Bactrian camel, with two. It's likely that Noah tried to squeeze quite a few camels into the Ark

Illus. 77. Project picture. The camel is about 4" from nose to tail and 3" high. Note that the grain needs to run up and down from the feet to the hump.

because, even though they are stubborn and obstinate animals, camels are also a swift and efficient means of transportation.

Although the camel in this project has one hump (Illus. 77), there's no reason why you couldn't give it two humps. Or, you could leave out the humps altogether and make a llama (Illus. 78). Regardless of how you modify this project in terms of humps, you should give this animal a long face, a long upward-curved neck, long legs, and big flat feet.

Take another look at Illus. 77 and see how the camel is slightly more difficult to carve than, say, the hippo, if only because the camel's neck and legs are so long. The problem isn't so much with the legs, per se, although they can be tricky, but since the grain of the wood needs to run up through the legs and consequently up through the neck, at the point where the neck meets the body the wood will tend to be short-grained and fragile. Therefore, you will have to choose your wood with extra care. As with the hippo project, it's a good idea to go for an easy-to-carve wood, such as lime; but when you come to selecting the particular piece, make a point of looking for a block that is especially smooth-grained and knot-free.

As with the other animal projects in the Berchtesgaden tradition, try to take a direct, primitive folk-art approach with this project. You don't need to achieve an anatomically correct carving, but to capture the basic characteristics that make up the naïve image we know to signify a camel.

Tools and Materials

For this project you need:
- a piece of 2" X 4" lime wood that is 4" long;
- a 2" X 3" piece of ¼"-thick wood for the base;
- a small straight saw—preferably a gents, but a tenon or even a large small-toothed crosscut will do;
- a coping saw with spare blades, or a small bow saw;
- a selection of knives, including a long fine-bladed whittling knife and a scalpel;
- a pencil and pad of work-out paper;
- a sheet of tracing paper;
- a pack of graded sandpapers;

Illus. 78. Inspirational drawing. Make note of other unusual beasts. Top left: African Bactrian camel. Top right: Australian kangaroo. Middle left: South American vicuna. Bottom left: African aardvark. Bottom right: South American llama.

- a small riffler file;
- four cans of enamel paint, in black, green, orange-brown, and yellow-brown;
- a can of primer;
- a can of white undercoat;
- a can of yacht varnish;
- a small quantity of hair, fur, or bristles;
- a selection of brushes;
- a measure;
- a set of callipers; and
- a workbench and a vise.

On the following page: Illus. 79. Working drawing. The scale is three grid squares to 1". See how, at the finishing stage, the hump is given a varnish-and-bristle texture.

73

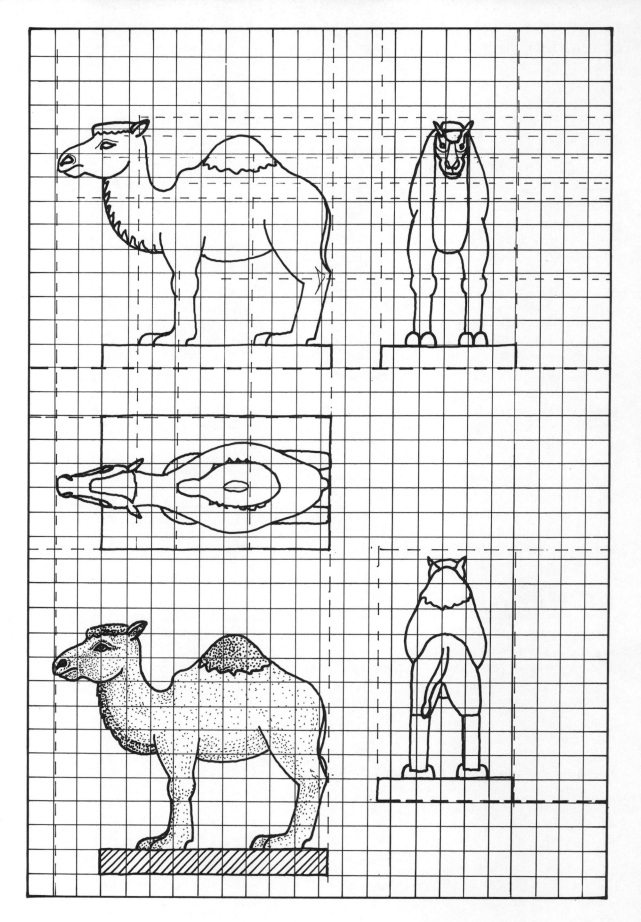

Setting Out the Design

First spend some time visiting the zoo, searching through books for pictures of camels, studying the illustrations that come with this project, looking at modern plastic-toy animals, making Plasticine models of camels, and generally becoming acquainted with different types of camels in all shapes and sizes. Then take a sheet of work-out paper, having another last look at the accompanying illustrations, and finalize your design. At this point in the project, don't work out details; just concentrate on the main lines of the form.

Set the 4" length of 2" × 4" lime out on the workbench so that the grain runs up and down and the cut end grain is uppermost, and then label the end-grain face *top* and the two 4" × 4" faces *side*. When you are sure that you have done this correctly, take a sheet of tracing paper and transfer the camel image through to one of the side faces. Now, draw in the profile with a soft pencil and shade in the areas of waste that need to be cut away.

Cutting the Side Profile and Roughing Out the Workpiece

This part of the project can be difficult, if only because the wood to be cut is 2" thick and the blades of the coping saw are flexible and fragile; so, take it slowly.

Secure the wood in the vise and start to fret out the profile. As you are sawing, keep the blade well to the waste side of the drawn line and try to hold the saw so that the angle between the side of the block and the sawn face stays at 90°.

As you are working, be prepared to reposition the wood in the vise and to maneuver the tool so that you can change the direction of the cut and obtain the best advantage. For example, when you are clearing away the waste from in front of the camel's neck and legs, start at the nose, cut down as far as the top of the leg, and then change tack and reposition the wood and cut in from the feet.

If you find this difficult, then it would be a good idea to take a small gents saw and make cuts that go in from the sides of the block and stop short when they reach critical points and angles around the

drawn outline. Then you can go back to using the coping saw, working around the profile, sawing from the end of one cut and on to the next. Gradually remove all the wedge-shaped areas of waste until you have fretted out the form (Illus. 80).

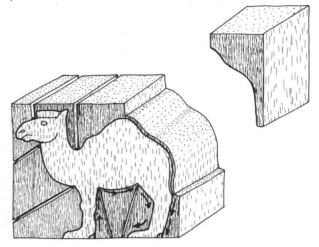

Illus. 80. First, draw the profile; next, use a straight saw to cut into the main dips, bumps, and humps; then, clear away the waste with a coping saw.

Establishing the Front, Top, and Back Views

Refresh your eye by looking at the accompanying drawings and the various views. Then take a pencil and shade in all the areas of waste on the sawn workpiece that are large enough to be worked with the coping saw (Illus. 81). You might shade in the area on each side of the head, the two wedge-shaped pieces on each side of the hump, the two U-shaped pieces from between the back and the front legs, and so forth.

If you have any doubts as to how the camel will look once you have wasted these areas, then quickly make a model with a block of Plasticine and take it through the various stages. This way, you can avoid making irreversible mistakes.

Of course, as with all other projects, before you make a cut you must check the direction and run of the grain. If necessary, modify the way the wood is held in the vise, as well as the pressure of your cut and the angle of the tool. Be warned, if you force or twist the tool through the grain, you will almost certainly split the wood.

Illus. 81. Left: Shade in the main blocks of waste, and then clear them away with the coping saw. Right: When the main blocks of waste have been cut away, identify the smaller areas of waste, such as both sides of the nose and between the toes; then saw them away in like manner.

Whittling and Finishing

When the main areas of rough have been cleared away, turn the now-recognizable camel over in your hands and compare it to the drawings of the camel. Take one of your stouter knives, and with the carving still cradled and supported in the palm of your hand, begin whittling away the rough-sawn faces (Illus. 82). Work from under the chin down to the top of the front legs, from the ears down to the base of the hump, and under and around the belly. Keep both the wood and the knife moving, working closer and closer to your envisioned form.

Of course, you will have to alter your cutting technique, depending on the stage that you are in and the part that you are carving. For example, when you are cutting from the belly down the legs towards the feet, you need to hold the knife in one hand while you push the blade away from yourself with the thumb of the other hand. But, when you are carving the hump, you need to pull the knife towards yourself with a single-handed thumb-supporting paring action. Essentially, your best approach is to change the type of cut and/or your tool to suit the job at hand.

If you remove the wood in small chips and curls, and do your best to avoid slicing directly and deeply into end grain, then you won't go far wrong. Good advice for a beginner is to cut across or with the grain, but never directly into it. But, when you have more or less roughed out the shape, take either a small fine-point penknife or a scalpel and start cutting in all the angles and details. Cut in the ears, the nostrils, the jaw, the slight suggestion of muscles at the top of the legs, the foot pads, the tail, and all the other characteristic details.

Now, with sandpaper, a riffler, a knife, and any other tools of your choice, work systematically backwards and forward over the carving, taking it to a smooth-to-the-touch finish. Don't overdo the rubbing down and thus spoil the beautifully crisp edges and angles left by the knives; just remove any roughness, untidy angles, and burrs.

Finally, clean up the little ¼"-thick piece of base wood, carefully rub the bottom of the foot pads on a sheet of sandpaper so that the camel will stand upright, and then glue the camel on the base.

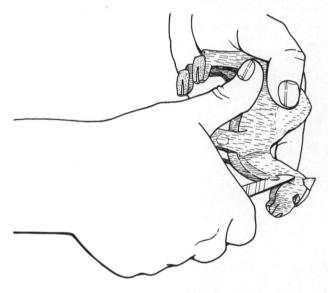

Illus. 82. Being careful not to let the blade run too deeply into fragile areas of grain, cradle the camel in one hand and gently whittle away with the knife held in the other. It's best to cut either across or at an angle to the grain.

Painting

When your carving is finished, clear away all your woodworking paraphernalia, remove all the wood dust with a vacuum cleaner, wipe the carving down with a turpentine-dampened cloth, and then set out all your paints and brushes so that they are easily within reach. Now is the time to stop and consider where you are going to keep your work once it has been painted. Are you going to put it up on a shelf? Are you going to leave it just where it is, and, if so, is it going to be in the way of children, pets, or your next project? Consider all these points and organize your work area accordingly.

When this is done, dip the camel first in the primer and then the undercoat, remembering to let the paint dry out between coats. Then, when the undercoat is dry, use a broad brush to apply an overall coat of brown-yellow. After a short while when the brown-yellow paint has dried somewhat, take either a small dry brush or a piece of clean cotton rag and carefully rub through certain painted areas so as to reveal some of the underlying white undercoat. This should create a hairlike texture. After a while, take a dryish brush and a little of the dark-brown paint and texture the camel's hump and feet, the area underneath the neck, and any other areas that you think need to look darker (Illus. 83).

Finally, paint the base green, dot in the eyes with black, give the whole piece a dip in the varnish, sprinkle a few hair clippings over the varnished hump, and the job is done.

Troubleshooting and Possible Modifications

• When you are making guide marks on the wood, always use a soft pencil. Never be tempted to use soft-tip pens since they bleed and stain.

• Use a white undercoat rather than the often-recommended muted shades. Then the white will shine through the top coat and give it a bit of a lift and sparkle.

• You can make the base with a scrap of superior-quality multi-core plywood.

• Ark camels have a small cord tail, which is glued into a small hand-drilled hole.

• If you neglect to clean up the wood dust before you start painting, when the dust settles it will fall on the painted animals and spoil your work.

Illus. 83. Prior to varnishing and bristling, use a dry brush to give the surface a scuffed hairlike texture.

Project 5
Whittling an Elephant in the Berchtesgaden Tradition

Design, Structure, and Technique Considerations

The Ark elephant is a real personality, and it's especially fun to carve, not only because of its big bold proportions, but also because of its asymmetrical trunk.

Take a look at Illus. 84–86 and see how the elephant's trunk curves in a full sweep down from its high-domed forehead and then tucks in and is attached to one side of its body. If you wish, you can modify the design and have the trunk curving up or hanging down; but, be warned, if you do decide to change the design, still try to have both ends of the trunk attached to the main body of the workpiece. We say this because if you made a loose-ended trunk, then you would undoubtedly have problems with weak short grain. Certainly, the elephant would look more dynamic if the trunk curved up, but unfortunately at several points along the curved-up section, the grain would be so short that the trunk would split off.

Traditionally, Ark characters needed to be as strong as possible so that they could withstand the wear and tear of children, and their design had to be simple and uncomplicated so that the carver could chop them out in a dozen or so swift, mechanical strokes. Bear such factors in mind when you are looking at Ark animals in toy museums and books and when you are considering profiles and views; then draw your designs accordingly.

Tools and Materials

For this project you need:
- a piece of 2 ½" X 4" lime wood that is 4" long;
- a 3" X 4" piece of ¼"-thick wood for the base;
- a small straight saw, such as a gents, keyhole, or pad saw;
- a coping or bow saw;
- a selection of knives;
- a pencil and a pad of work-out paper;
- tracing paper;
- a pack of graded sandpapers;
- a good-size piece of Plasticine;
- a small riffler file;
- a hand drill with a small drill bit;
- PVA wood glue;
- three cans of enamel paint in green, grey, and red-pink;
- a can of primer;
- a can of white undercoat;
- a can of yacht varnish;
- a selection of brushes; and

- the usual workshop items, such as a workbench and vise, turpentine, paint containers, stirring sticks, newspapers, and old cloths.

Making a Model

This project is tricky and at the same time easy. It can be difficult to make the Plasticine model and to figure out the asymmetrical placement of the trunk, but once the details have been established, then the actual carving is relatively straightforward.

There are two ways you can go about making the model: You can either add pieces to the basic body lump and build the model up and out, or you can cut and remove pieces—taking the Plasticine through the "carving" stages. For this project, it is best to use the latter method.

Take the Plasticine and knock it into a 2 ½" X 4" X 4" brick shape. When this is done, take a tracing from your master design and press the lines of the profile through to the 4" X 4" side face of the Plasticine. Now, with the full knowledge that if anything goes wrong, you can simply stick the Plasticine back together and start over again, set about "carving" the form. Swiftly establish the big broad back, the sturdy legs, and the belly (Illus. 87). Then concentrate your efforts on shaping the ears, forehead, and trunk. Make the ears pinned back against the side of the head, and make the trunk come down in a smooth curve so that it tucks into either the right or left side of the chest.

When you feel that the model is finished, slowly turn it around, just to make sure that each view has an interesting feature. Finally, clear away all the extra bits and pieces of Plasticine, place the model on a dais so that it is out of harm's way but within easy reach, pin up your drawings and other inspirational material, and arrange your tools so that they are close at hand.

Illus. 84. Project picture. The elephant is about 4" long from head to tail and 4" high. Note how the trunk curves down and to one side.

Illus. 85. Inspirational drawing. Looking for other animals with unusual tusks, trunks, and noses? Top: African elephant. Middle: South American giant anteater. Second from bottom: elephant seal. Bottom: walrus.

Making Your First Cuts

Once you have made a model and thus sorted out most of the design and form problems, label your chosen block of wood *side, top,* and *front,* and then, with a pencil, press-transfer the lines of the traced profile through to one of the side faces. If all is well, the elephant should approximately fit the 4" X 4" area.

Secure the wood in the vise and use either the bow saw or the coping saw to swiftly clear away the small corners of waste and the larger U-shaped piece under the belly. When this has been done, take the hand drill and bit and work a pilot hole through the small enclosed "window" of waste that occurs be-

tween the trunk and the body (Illus. 88). Now, unhitch the blade from the coping saw, pass it through the pilot hole, retension the blade in its frame, and start to cut away the waste.

Working a small area of enclosed waste is simple enough as long as you remember to hold the saw so that the blade is at right angles to the flat face of the profile, keep the saw blade on the waste side of the drawn lines, and speed up the sawing action at the corners and sharp bends. Be warned, if you slow up at the corners, try to backtrack, or try to change the direction of the cut while the saw is still, you will probably break the blade.

Whittling and Modelling the Trunk and Head

Once you have removed the waste from the profile, stand the block of wood so that you can see it from the front. Take another look at Illus. 86, and then take a pencil and sketch in the lines of the front view. Noting how the width of the profile allows for the trunk to swing either to the left or the right, settle for one side or the other and sketch it in.

Now, take a good sharp knife, and, being aware of the run of the grain, cut back the waste wood around the trunk until you reach the elephant's chest. It's simple enough to remove the wood on the trunk's outer curve, but when you come to removing the waste on the top or the inside curve, then you do have to work with caution. Start by defining the area of waste with a few V-section stop cuts; then clean out and lower the wood to the depth of the cuts. As long as you redefine the area and depth of the piece to be wasted at each level, you should be all right. Work at a nice gentle pace—checking back with the design, cutting in a stop cut, lowering the wood, rubbing the knife on the sharpening stone, reworking the stop cut, carving a little more, and so on. When you have lowered the wood on all sides of the trunk, take a smaller sharper knife to the now-squarish trunk and whittle off the corners. Now, with one eye on the model and the other on the run of the grain, slide the razor-sharp knife through the

On the opposite page: Illus. 86. Working drawing. The scale is about three grid squares to 1".

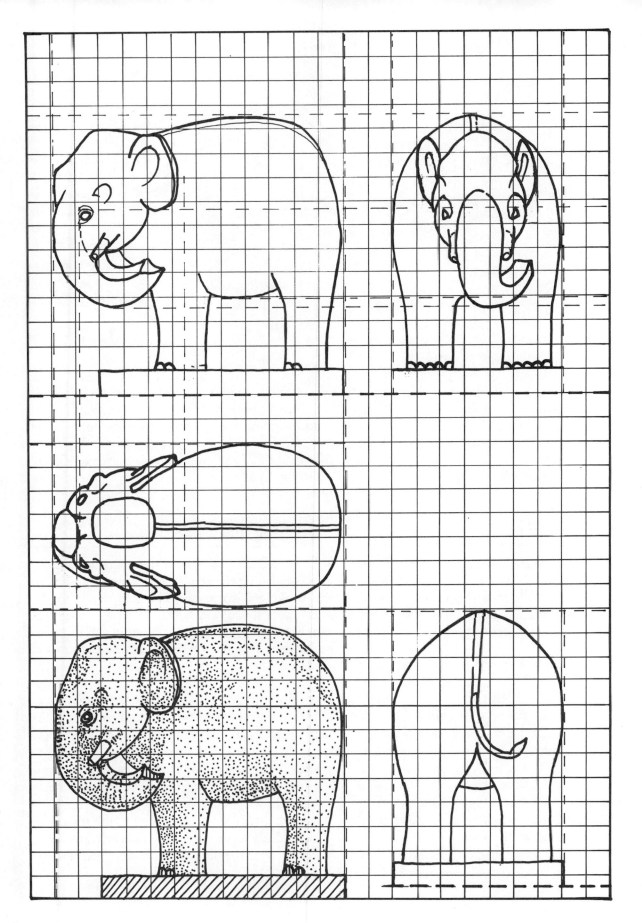

81

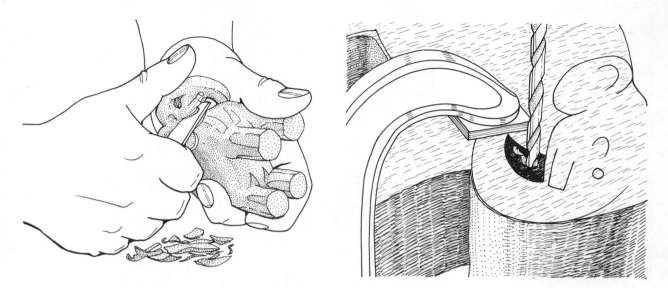

Illus. 87 (left). When you make your Plasticine model, be sure to establish the big, bold curves. Illus. 88 (right). Once you have sawn out the form as seen in the side view, use a drill and coping saw to clear away the area of enclosed-trunk waste.

small angles and corners of waste wood, gradually working towards a full and rounded trunklike shape.

When this is done, take the knife to the upper part of the forehead, cut away the side-to-front corners, and then gradually work towards creating the characteristic, rather top-heavy, massive, high-domed form.

Modelling the Ears

Holding the elephant so that you can see it from the side, take a soft pencil and draw in the large C-shaped ear. When this is done, cut the line of the C into the wood to a depth of about ⅛", and work two side-by-side angled cuts so as to make a V-shaped trench (Illus. 89).

Using this V-section trench as a knife block or stop cut, slice away and lower the surrounding wood so that the C is left in high-relief. In other words, working on the waste side of the C, skim the blade through the waste and into the stop cut so as to remove a thin layer. Continue in this manner, first establishing and defining the C-shape with a stop cut, and then lowering the waste around the ear to the depth of the cut. You should lower the wood above and behind the ear until there is at least a ¼" step down from the rim of the ear to the body.

Now, take a razor-sharp scalpel or penknife to the

rim of the ear and very carefully remove slivers of wood from above and below the rim until it looks round and undercut. Finally, take the knife to the large flat face of the ear and begin gradually removing small scoops of wood. Try to carve a delicate dished form that faces towards an off-center ear hole. Carve both ears in like manner.

Modelling and Finishing

When you have established the main lines of the form—meaning the profile, trunk, and ears—place the workpiece on a dais and compare it to the drawings and your Plasticine model. Let your eyes run over the form, noting its qualities and its faults, and, if necessary, go over it with a knife and remodel certain areas.

Now, take the knife to the side-to-sawn-edge corners of the legs, belly, back, and rump, and proceed to work them to a smooth roundness. As with the other animals, try to work with, at an angle to, or across the grain—but never directly into or against it (Illus. 90). For example, when you carve the legs, the knife is worked from the belly down towards the foot; when you work the back, the knife is slid from the flank up and over to the top of the back; and when you carve the underbelly, the knife is worked from the flank downwards. As to whether

Illus. 89. Top left: Outline the shape of the ear with a V-section trench. Top right: Lower the wood around the ear. Bottom left: Round off the square-cut rim of the ear. Bottom right: Model and "dish" the inside of the ear.

or not you are carving efficiently, let the shape and character of each cut be your guide. Ideally, the knife should slip into the wood, leaving it looking butter-smooth, shiny, and slightly scoop-textured, or dappled. If the wood cuts up rough or ragged, then it's likely that you are cutting against the grain or that the wood is unsuitably resinous or knotty; then, again, perhaps your knives simply need sharpening.

When you feel that your carving is finished, take your sharpest and finest scalpel and go over the wood, cutting in the angles and embellishing the surface with dappled tool marks. Then use the sandpaper and riffler file on all the difficult corners, and cut in the eyes, work a few creases on the inside curve of the trunk, detail the end of the trunk and the feet, and generally go over the entire workpiece. Finally, rub the feet down on sandpaper and glue the elephant in place on the base.

Painting

As with all the other projects, before you start painting spend some time clearing away all the bench clutter, cleaning up all the dust, wiping the

workpiece with a cloth, setting out your paints and brushes, and deciding where you are going to place the elephant once it has been painted.

As soon as your work area is organized, use a broad soft-haired brush and, remembering to let the paint dry out between coats, apply a generous coat of

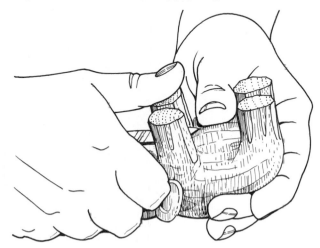

Illus. 90. If possible, avoid cutting directly into end grain. For example, when you come to carving the belly and inside-leg areas, run the knife across the belly, around the angle of the leg-and-belly area, and down the leg.

83

primer and an undercoat. When the undercoat is dry (this might take anything up to 8 hours, depending upon temperature and air flow), take your finest knife and trim off any runs and blobs. Now, take a small fine-point brush and paint the body gray, the base green, and the details of the eyes, mouth, and trunk tip red-pink. Finally, apply a generous coat of varnish and let it dry, and then introduce Jumbo to his friends.

Troubleshooting and Possible Modifications

• If your wood cuts up ragged—even though it is, say, a choice piece of lime and you have spent hours sharpening your knives—there's a chance that the wood is sappy. When this is the case, dry it out slightly and try again.

• If your wood is knotty and resinous, coat it with a sealer before you start painting.

• If, by chance, you split off some part of the carving, you can bond the parts with a resin glue, leave it overnight, and then start up where you left off.

• Before you start painting, the workpiece must be well-prepared and free from dust, splinters, and greasy fingerprints. Be careful not to mix paints of a different brand or type. If you have any doubts regarding your paint, take a piece of scrap wood through all the painting stages.

• If you want the animals to be larger or smaller than the project specifies, simply change the scale of the working drawing grid (Illus. 86). For example, although, at our scale of three grid squares to 1", the elephant comes out about 4" high, 4" long, and 2 ½" wide, there's no reason why you couldn't change the scale to, say, six grid squares to 1", enlarge the working drawings, and finish up with a big push-along toy elephant that is 8" high and 8" long.

3
THE ERZGEBIRGE ARK

The Erzgebirge Ark (Illus.91, and Illus. 3 on page C in the color section) has got to be seen to be believed. Measuring about 24" from prow to stern, wonderfully decorated with colored flat-straw marquetry, full to the gunwales with about 90 pairs of animals and eight turned and carved figures, it is undoubtedly the most visually exciting of all the Arks.

When we first saw one in a museum, we were told that it was made by French prisoners of war, meaning that it was made in England sometime between 1799 and 1815 when soldiers captured during the Napoleonic wars were allowed to earn money at their trades. We knew that it was on record that French prisoners did plait straw for the hat trade, but we had never heard mention of them making or decorating Arks. So, even though this particular Ark was described as being made by the French, and despite the fact that it has an intricacy that is characteristically French, we still had a hunch that it was German because the figures and animals looked German to us. Well, sure enough, after a great deal of searching about in museums and old book shops, we are now absolutely certain that this type of highly decorative straw-work Ark is German—or, to be more precise, that it originated in the Erzgebirge mountains, on the East German Czechoslovakian border, during the nineteenth century.

Even more interesting, perhaps, is the fact that we also now know these Arks to be the result of an almost inevitable coming together of several woodcraft traditions. The villages in the Erzgebirge area have a long tradition of making beautifully decorative wood wares. For instance, the Grunhainichen woodworkers were sending wooden toys to America as far back as 1770, and the Seiffen woodworkers and turners were making delicate boxes and all manner of other brightly painted and highly decorative wares as long ago as 1800. The Erzgebirge Ark can be seen as the successful culmination of all these craft traditions.

Although it is known that in about 1790, in Erzgebirge and Thuringia, boxed farms, menageries, and towns—meaning wood-carved trees, houses, people, and animals, all packed into slide-lid boxes—were commonly made, it is not known who first had the idea of pooling the skills of a whole range of woodworkers and packaging the animals in boat-shaped boxes and calling them Arks. Probably sometime in the first half of the nineteenth century when Erzgebirge toy makers were exporting large numbers of such toys to America and when shipping costs were often prohibitively expensive, someone thought of miniaturizing the carved animals and redesigning the slat-wood shipping crates. What had once been just a random collection of carved animals and figures, all packed into a throwaway shipping crate, now became a selection of Ark figures and animals packed into an Ark.

Illus. 91. The Erzgebirge Ark is about 24" from prow to stern, 20" high, and 8" wide. Note the applied marquetry and the high prow and stern boards.

86

Project 1
Making an Ark in the Erzgebirge Tradition

Design and Structure Considerations

Start by looking at the Erzgebirge Ark in Illus. 91 and the one shown in the color section, and note how it is barrel-, or cooper-, built using vertical strips, or staves, and also see how the whole structure appears to be covered with decorative, multicolored laid-, or flat-, straw marquetry. As you can see, this Ark is tricky on two counts: Firstly, it is quite a complicated form to build, and, secondly, once built, the marquetry designs need to be worked with delicacy and precision.

Because of its relative complexity, you must decide right from the start how you are going to approach the project. For example, are you going to follow the traditional Erzgebirge techniques and only work with strip pine and straw? Or, are you going to update the project and build a plywood carcass and then cover it with straw? Spend some time weighing the pros and cons of different materials and techniques, and then plan the design and structure accordingly.

Now, take a look at the rest of the accompanying illustrations and see how, although we have decided to cooper-build our Ark in the traditional manner using 1/2"-thick slats, or staves, we have nevertheless decided to modify the decorative technique and use colored wood veneers rather than straw. Certainly, as traditionalists, we would have liked to have used straw, but we just couldn't find a supplier. . . .

At first sight the designs may look complex, but they are, in fact, relatively simple and straightforward. For instance, with the band of pattern that runs around the house, just under the eaves, the little squares of color may look as if they were applied individually but they were actually worked as a sheet. Vertical colored strips of wood veneer were mounted on a backing paper, cut horizontally, and then shifted so that the colors produced a vertical counterchange. All the bands of pattern, including the angled pattern around the roof and the one under the windows, were worked using this type of simple parquetry technique.

After having carefully looked over the drawings, if you still have any doubts as to how to work the parquetry techniques, then take some scraps of colored paper and experiment with the various cut-and-shift methods, as illustrated.

Tools and Materials

For this project you need:
- at least 16 square feet of 1/2"-thick strip, or slat,

wood, meaning a selection of pieces ½" thick, 1"–4" wide, and up to 28" long;

- a good selection of wood veneers, in colors and strip sizes to suit the project;
- a tenon saw;
- a set square;
- a Surform rasp;
- a small hammer;
- a cutting board and metal straightedge;
- PVA wood glue;
- contact adhesive that is suitable for wood veneers;
- a sponge;
- a cabinet scraper;
- a roll of brown-paper reinforced carton-sealing tape;
- a measure;
- a quantity of ¾" brass brads;
- a pad of work-out paper;
- a ¼"-wide straight chisel;
- grain sealer;
- a craft knife;
- a pack of graded sandpapers;
- wax polish; and
- all the usual workshop items, such as newspaper, cloths, and pencils.

Building the Hull Carcass

Take a look at Illus. 94 and see how this Ark is really no more than a slant-sided, round-ended cooper-built box. There is a base and a main deck, both of which are built from strips that run the length of the boat. And with the base and deck used as formers, the sides of the Ark are built from strips that run vertically from the base to the deck. Note how the cooper technique allows for a certain amount of trial and error in placing the various elements that make up the design.

Start by establishing the shape of the base and the main deck; draw the two shapes on newspaper and then cut them out with a pair of scissors. Now, using the paper templates as a guide, place the various strips on the work surface, making sure that they run from the prow to the stern, allow for the main hatchway, being sure that the side edges of the strips butt together for a good fit, and then prepare to work with the hammer, brass brads, and glue. First, smear glue along all the butting side edges; then place the

battens across the strips, and finally nail through the strips into the battens. When the glue is dry, take the rasp to the edges of the two forms, and work them to a good, round-ended, smooth-lined profile. You should now have two round-ended forms: the base at about 18" long and 6" wide, and the main deck at about 24" long and a little less than 8" wide (refer to Illus. 93).

When you have made the base and deck, take another look at the pertinent drawings and note that the sides of the Ark measure about 8" from the base to the deck at the lowest point and about 12" from the base to the gunwale at the prow and stern, and then start cutting the wood to size.

When you are ready to frame up the hull, first establish the deck-to-base level by attaching four 8"-long temporary battens, two on each side of the hull, as shown in Illus. 94. Now, starting at the center of the sides, work out and around towards the prow and stern, cutting, gluing, and nailing the vertical hull strips as you go. Allowing plenty of extra length for the strips, chamfer all the butting sides to a good fit, working out from both sides so as to meet at the center of the prow and stern. If you work as described, you will find that the strips, or slats, can be anything up to 4" wide at the sides, but as you build around the curve of the prow and stern, you will find that you need to use very narrow strips and to chamfer their edges until they are almost triangular in sections.

When you have worked all the way around the hull and fitted and adjusted the final prow and stern keel strips, wait for the glue to dry and then take a saw and rasp, and work along the top edge of the hull, cutting back and shaping the gunwales.

Building the House Carcass

After you've made the hull, take a look at the drawings and consider the size and shape of the

On the following pages: Illus. 92. Cutting grid. The scale is about one grid square to 2". Note that the Ark is built up from ½"-thick slats. Illus. 93. Working drawing. Top: The scale is one grid square to 2". Middle: The sections are not to scale. Note the sliding-door section; see how the top of the door slides under the roof eaves, while the bottom runs in a groove in the deck.

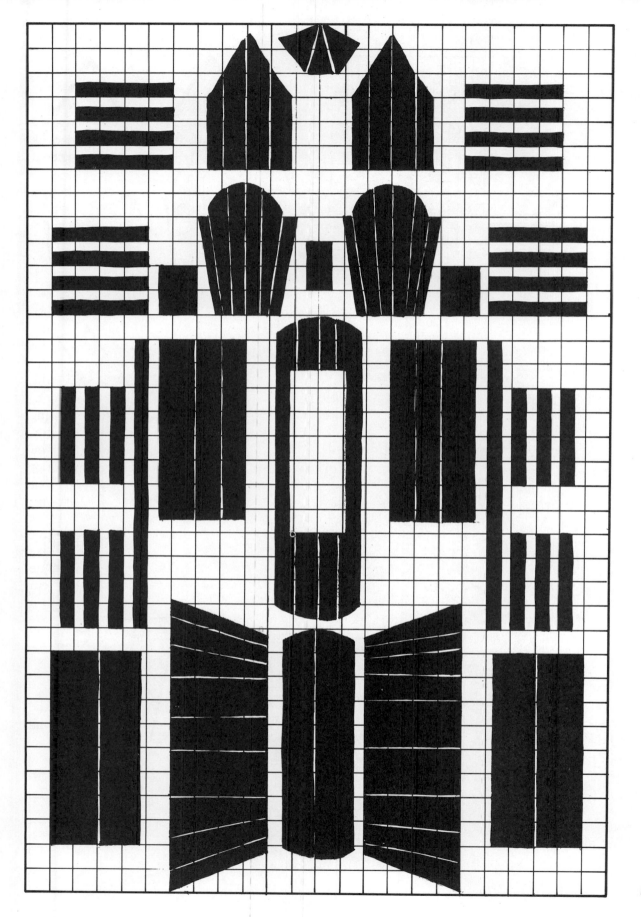

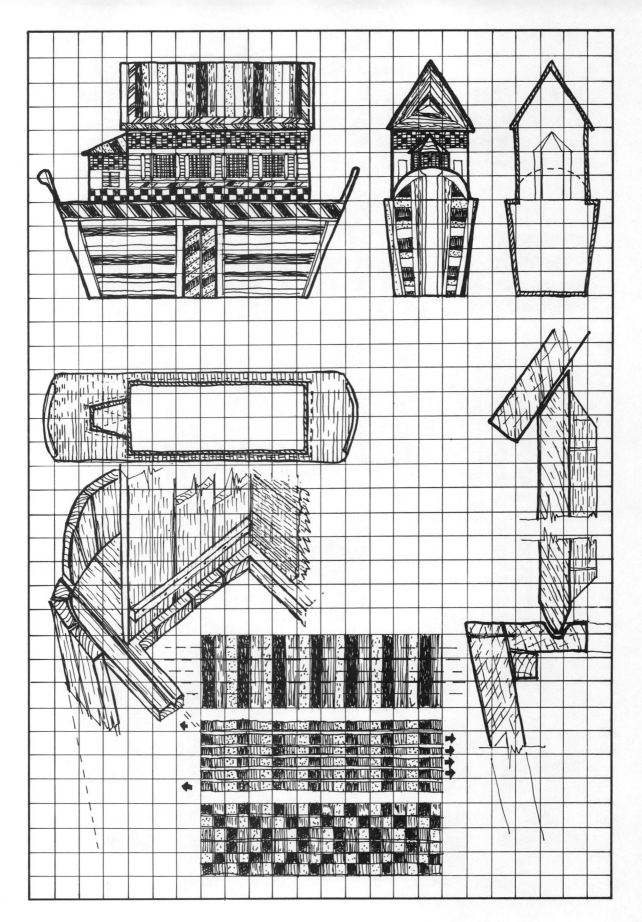

house—meaning the height of the walls, the pitch of the roof, and the way the little porch fits at the prow. Note that, with this design, one complete side wall also functions as a sliding door. See how the top edge of this side wall fits under the eaves of the roof and slots into the deck. Once you have noted all the measurements, make three paper templates: one for a long side wall, one for an end-gable wall, and one for the roof.

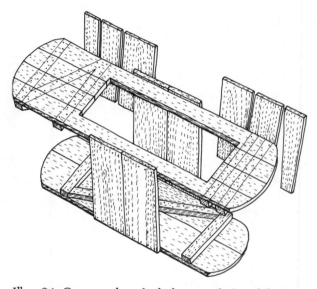

Illus. 94. Once you have built the main deck and the base, use them as formers, and fit and attach the vertical slats. See how the decks are "Z"-braced.

When this is done, clear the work surface and set out the wood for the long, fixed side wall. Arrange the various strips so that they run along the length of the house, set the battens so that they run from the deck to the eaves, and then glue and batten-attach, as already described for the main deck and the base. Now, build both gable walls in a like manner, only make the strips run vertically. When this is done, arrange the three walls so that you have, as it were, a house with one long side wall and two end-gable walls. Position this three-sided structure over the main-deck hatchway so that the long wall is set back slightly from the edge of the deck. If you've done this correctly, you should be able to place the house over the hatchway so that when the wall that opens is attached, it can slide back along the deck, just clearing the rising curve of the gunwale. If necessary, adjust the size of the house by

cutting back or increasing the width of the gable walls.

When you have established the exact position of the house and consequently the route of the long sliding door, use the tenon saw and the straight chisel to cut the deck track. Cut two parallel saw kerfs about 1/4" apart and the full length of the deck; then use the straight chisel to lower the wood between the two cuts.

Now, build the two sides of the roof the way you built the walls, and then have a trial fitting of the roof and, if necessary, adjust it to fit.

When you come to building the wall that slides back, cut, glue, and batten-attach, as already described, only this time make the top edge a tight fit under the roof eaves and the bottom edge a smooth-running fit in the deck track (Illus. 95). If you think it's necessary to strengthen the door, attach a single vertical batten at the center of the back. Make sure that the ends of the batten are chamfered, cut back, and well clear of both the deck track and the eaves; then check to see that as the door opens, the batten acts as a door stop. The door should slide open, either to the left or to the right, to reveal an opening that is about 6"–7" wide.

When you are happy with the way the door slides, then glue the house to the main deck, and the roof to the walls. When this is done, cut the five little pieces that go into making up the porch, and then

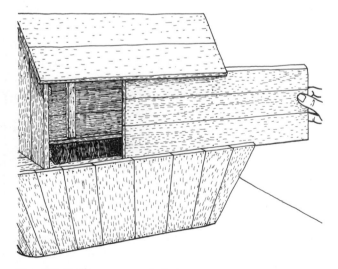

Illus. 95. Before you attach the house to the main deck, make sure that the long wall is a smooth-sliding fit between the eaves and the deck groove.

build the porch on the house wall at the prow of the Ark.

Now, make sure that the door still opens; if necessary, trim back the prow and stern walls. Then go over the whole structure with the graded sandpapers, bringing it to a good, smooth finish.

The Parquetry—Considerations and Initial Steps

First, clear away all the clutter—such as the scraps of wood, large tools, and sawdust—and set out the veneers, contact adhesive, cutting board, straightedge, the brown-paper carton-sealing tape, and knives. Now, look at Illus. 96 and see how the parquetry technique involves cutting thin strips of veneer, setting them side by side, recutting, rearranging, taping, recutting, resetting, and so on. Technically, parquetry differs from marquetry only in that the designs and motifs are interlocking and geometrical rather than floral. See how by cutting, reversing, and alternating color sequences, you can achieve any number of attractive designs and motifs.

Now, starting with the simple checker strip around the bottom of the house, select two veneers that will produce a light-and-dark contrast. For example, you might want to use sycamore and red padauk, or birch and rosewood—whatever you use, just make sure that the two woods contrast. Then decide on the size of the checker squares. For example, if you want yours to be ½" X ½", then with the pencil, metal straightedge, and craft knife, slice the veneer sheets down so that you have a number of ½"-wide strips. Now, carefully arrange the strips side by side, with the two colors alternating, check for a good edge-to-edge fit, and then use the tape to stick the strips together (Illus. 97).

The Parquetry—Cross-Cutting and Creating the Design

When the tape is dry, use a set square to square off one strip-end edge of the composite sheet; then work down the sheet and across the grain, cutting off ½"-wide strips. Now, take the strips of contrasting light and dark veneer, and butt them edge to edge so

as to create the checker design. When you have built a two-line sequence, making sure that the colors are alternating, use the brown-paper carton-sealing tape to attach the two strips edge to edge. Continue in this manner with all the other designs—cutting veneer strips, arranging the strips side by side, taping, recutting at various angles, and so on, until you have a stockpile of all the patterned composite sheets that make up the total design (Illus. 98).

Applying, Gluing, and Pressing the Veneer

Once you have prepared the veneer sheets as described and collected all the small filler pieces, take a damp cloth and go over the Ark, wiping up all the wood dust.

Now, take the made-up composite sheet of veneer for a particular area, place it tape-side out against the Ark, and mark it to size with a hard pencil. Use a steel ruler and a craft knife to cut it to size. When this is done, check just to make sure that you have the pattern running in the right direction, and then spread a thin even layer of contact adhesive on both the face of the Ark and the veneer. Now, using the greatest of care and caution, bring the two sticky faces together, strap the veneer in position with carton-sealing tape, and then go on to the next area to be covered (Illus. 99).

Continue in this manner, gradually covering the Ark with the veneer. Of course, as you go, you will have to fill in spots and generally correct mistakes, but don't worry because this is as it should be.

Finishing

When you have finished covering the areas with veneer, wait until the glue is completely dry, and then take a sponge and as little water as possible, and dampen the Ark; then remove the tape.

When this is done, take the cabinet scraper and

On the opposite page: Illus. 96. Parquetry grid. This is not to scale. See how the five pattern arrangements are read and worked from left to right. For example, with the arrangement on the top, the strips of veneer are first arranged and attached vertically, the sheet is cut horizontally, and then the horizontal strips are staggered and attached.

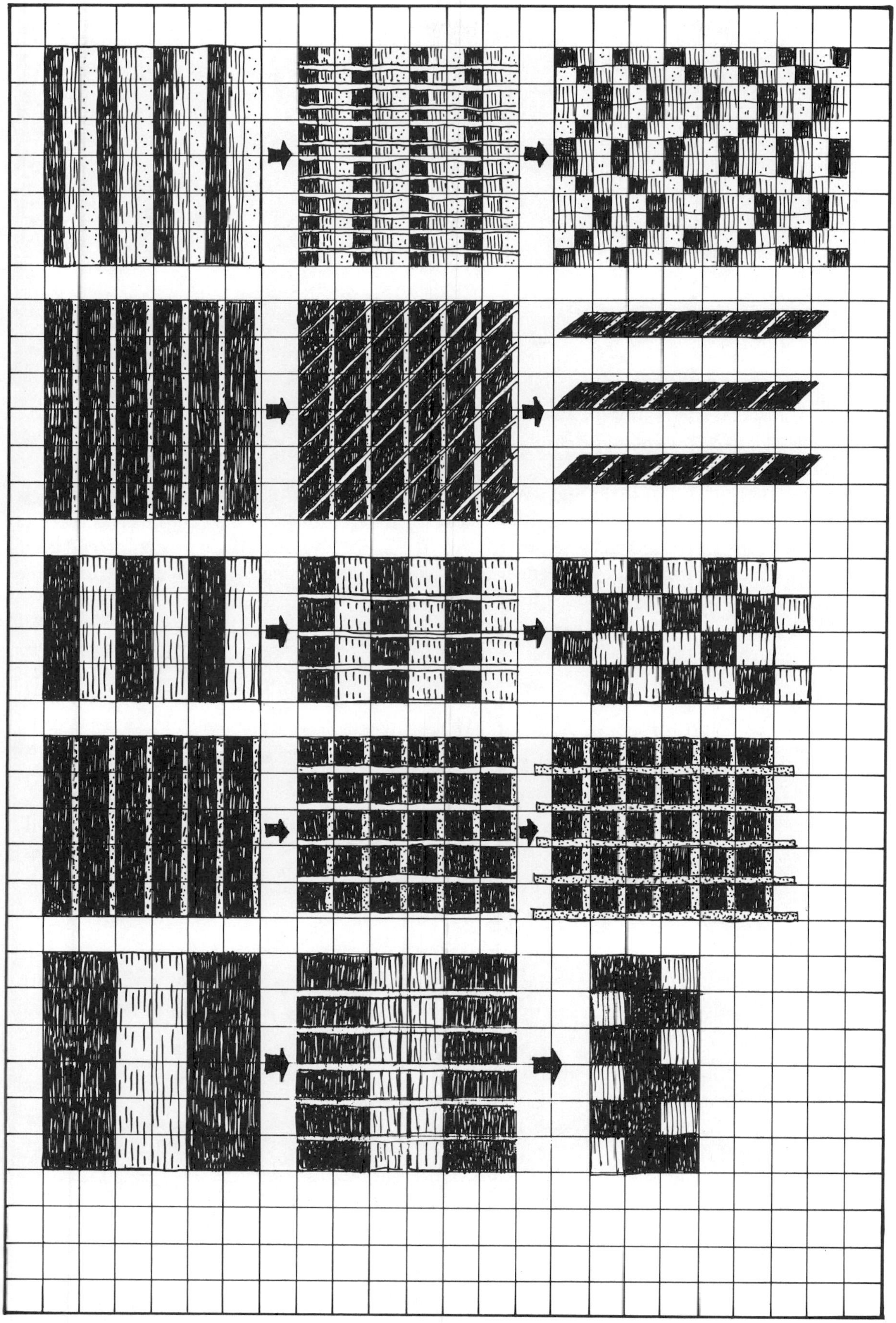

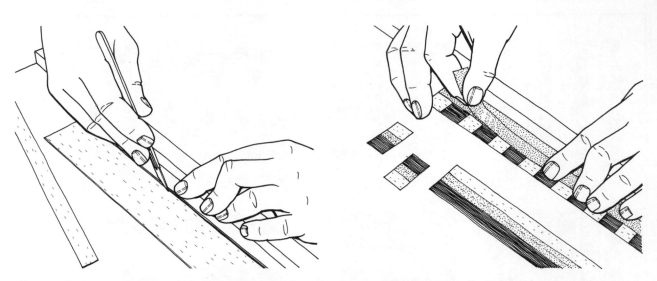

Illus. 97 (left). Cut the various-colored veneers into ½"-wide strips, and then tape them together edge to edge. Illus. 98 (right). Cut across the edge-to-edge colored strips, and then rearrange them according to your design plan.

work the face of the veneer until it looks and feels reasonably smooth (Illus. 100). Now, give the entire surface of the Ark a coat of grain sealer. When the sealer is dry, work through the range of graded sandpapers—starting with the rough and ending with the superfine—rubbing down the entire outside of the Ark until it feels completely smooth to the touch. Finally, take a plain wax polish and a fine cotton cloth and bring the veneer parquetry to a burnished finish.

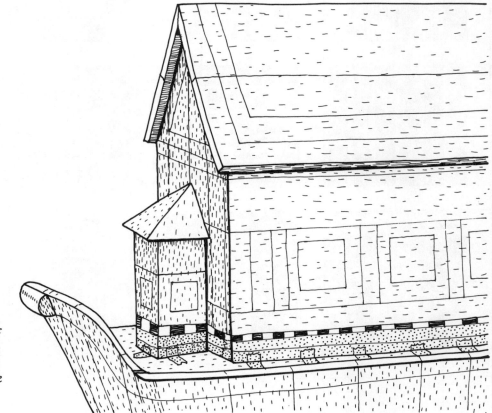

Illus. 99. Mark out the various design blocks, such as the windows and the plinth. Smear a thin layer of contact adhesive on both the veneer and the surface to be decorated. Then position the veneer and hold it in place with a strip of tape.

94

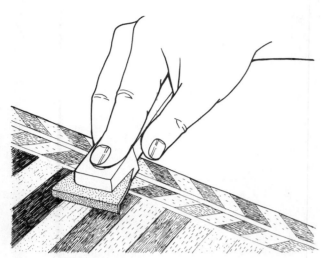

Illus. 100. Once the glue is dry, remove the tape and use a cabinet scraper to work the veneer to a good, smooth finish.

Troubleshooting and Possible Modifications

• When you are choosing the wood for the carcass, try to find wood that is smooth and knot-free and resistant to splitting.

• When you are selecting veneers, try to stay away from brittle, difficult-to-cut burrs. It's best to use soft, smooth-grained, easy-to-work veneers.

• If you are a beginner, consider using iron-on adhesive film rather than contact adhesive, even though it's more expensive.

• After you've built the carcass, you might reinforce the interior angles with off cuts bedded in glue.

• If you want a hard-wearing, knock-proof finish, use yacht varnish rather than wax.

Project 2
Making a Lathe-Turned Figure in the Erzgebirge Tradition

Design, Structure, and Technique Considerations

Erzgebirge Ark figures are so subtle and cleanly worked that it's hard to believe that they had their beginnings during a grim mining slump in the eighteenth century. But that's the way it was. Certainly, the whole mountainous and heavily forested area around Seiffen and Heidelberg always had a strong woodworking tradition, and, so, it was likely that the miners in this area made whittled and turned playthings for their children. But it wasn't until a post-war depression killed off the tin trade and forced the mines to close that the unemployed miners set their lathes up in the unused tin-stamping mills and started to turn wooden toys in earnest.

As to the origin of the design of the little turned and carved Ark figures, the turners might have copied the stamped-tin figures that were being made in Nurnberg at about that time, or they could have drawn inspiration from the paper-pulp figures that were being made in Thuringia. However, it is also just as likely that the design of the figures grew directly out of the wood-turning process. With this idea in mind, take a good look at the accompanying illustrations and note how the figures are really no more than very simple skittle dolls. See how with a few cuts of the knife, and a little bit of turning and carving, a basic turned shape can be easily transformed into a delightful little figure. If you slice away a bit of wood here and add a little glued beard there, a turned skittle will become a Mr. Noah; or, if you suggest a full dress and a nicely rounded bosom, the same turning will become a Mrs. Noah (Illus. 101). Such small turned figures that have been minimally worked with the knife and built up with carved and whittled additions are at the heart of the Noah's Ark tradition.

Take a look at the working drawings (Illus. 102 and 103), and see how at six grid squares to 1", the little turned figures stand about 3 to 4" high from the bottom of the bases to the top of the brimmed hats. Also, note how Mr. Noah has been knife-worked at the chest and back, how Mrs. Noah has only been knife-worked at the back, how Mr. Noah has an added beard, and how they both have added stick legs, bases, hats, noses, and peg-attached arms.

Of course, from village to village this type of turned Ark figure often varied—some were taller than others and some were brightly patterned, had pivotted arms that moved, had hats and bodies that were all of a piece, had staffs and backpacks, and so on—but each variation held true to the same traditional skittle-turned form. Therefore, if you want to

Illus. 101. Project picture. Mr. and Mrs. Noah are 3" to 4" high. Note the stick legs, Mr. Noah's added beard, and the way the arms are dowelled and attached.

make authentic Ark figures, you can modify small details, but it's important for you to stay within the overall naïve simplicity of the imagery. If you want to make museum look-alikes, don't overwork the carving, don't use complex secondary colors, and don't overdo the painted face details.

Before you begin this project, visit a folk museum, study the various traditional forms of turned toys and figures, and spend some time drawing characteristic profiles and details. Then read the sections on turning and note how the main components that make up the figure are all turned off, from left to right, as a single piece. Finally, note that although this project only gives directions for making Mrs. Noah, you can easily modify the details to make the rest of the family.

Tools and Materials

For this project you need:
- a piece of 1½" × 1½" squared wood that's 6" long—it's best to choose a good turning wood, such as ash, beech, holly, lime, or a fruit wood;
- a set of turning gouges, including a skew chisel and a ½" scraper;
- the use of a small wood lathe;
- a center punch;
- callipers;
- a pair of compasses/dividers;
- a small plane or rasp;
- a small straight saw;
- a coping saw;
- a hand drill with ⅛", ⅜", and ¼" drill bits;
- acrylic wood primer;
- acrylic paints, in colors to suit the project;
- varnish;
- a good selection of brushes; and
- all the usual woodworking/toy-making items, such as a bench with a vise, sandpaper, knives, a pencil, a measure, and glue.

Turning Off the Basic Cylinder

First, make sure that the lathe is in good working order and that the tools are conveniently within reach but out of harm's way. Now, select your 1½" × 1½" squared 6"-long piece of wood and check it over, just to make sure that it is smooth-grained and free from flaws, such as knots, splits, and stains. If you are a beginner or if you are planning on making several figures, then you might as well prepare a little stockpile of wood pieces.

With a measure, pencil, pair of compasses or dividers, square, and saw, square off each end of the wood and set each end out with a 1"-diameter circle. Mark off the corners of waste and then use a plane to swiftly work the wood down to a 6"-long octagonal section.

On the following pages: Illus. 102 (left). Working drawing for Mrs. Noah. The scale is about six grid squares to 1". Note the rod-and-spigot attachment of the various additions—the hat to the head, the arms to the body, and the legs to the base. Illus. 103 (right). Working drawing for Mr. Noah. The scale is about six grid squares to 1".

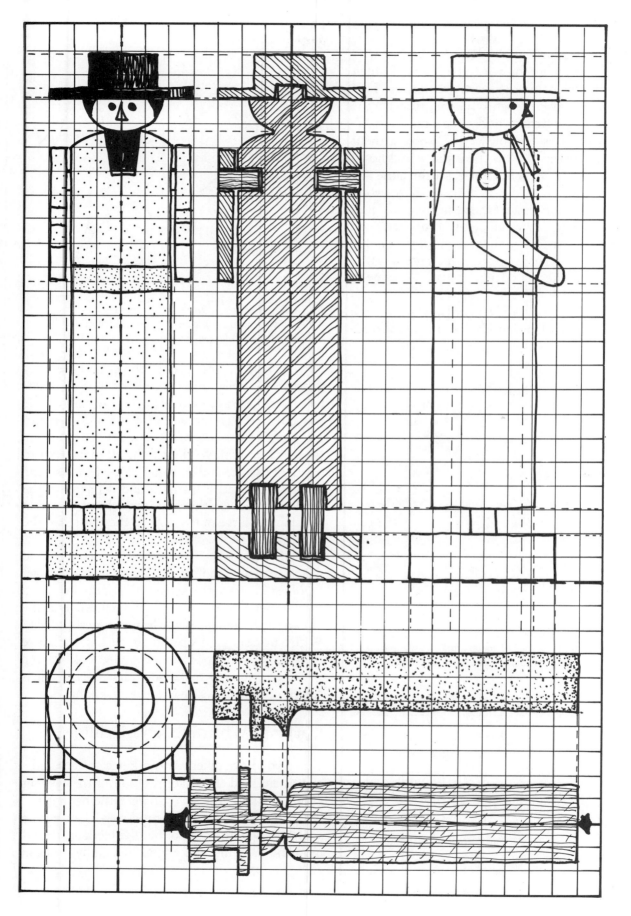

When this is done, establish the end centers with the punch and mount the wood on the lathe. Tighten up the tailstock so that the lathe centers run hard into the wood, ease off slightly, making sure that the wood is secure, and then check to be sure that the T-rest is as close as possible to the wood without actually touching it. Now, take the round-nosed chisel, or the tool of your choice, set the lathe at a fast speed, switch it on, and then set to work, stripping away the waste. Once you have achieved a round section, set the callipers to 1" diameter and use the parting tool to cut in a couple of pilot holes. Lower and waste the wood at the pilot holes so that at that point the cylinder is a tight 1"-diameter calliper fit.

Once you have worked two or three such depth guides, use the tools of your choice to work the piece down to an overall 1" diameter (Illus. 104).

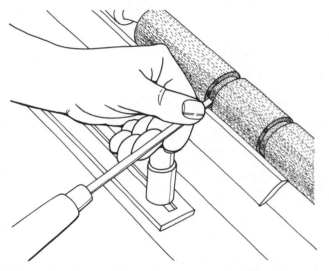

Illus. 104. Secure the wood centered on the lathe, cut in a couple of pilot slots to a 1" diameter, and waste the wood to the depth of the slots so as to make a 1"-diameter cylinder.

Turning the Profile

When you have achieved a smooth-faced 1"-diameter cylinder, take a pencil and a ruler and mark out along the length of the wood the position of all the necks and hollows (Illus. 105). Carefully check these points off against the appropriate working drawing, and, when you are sure that all your marks are correct, take a parting tool and cut in to the required depth.

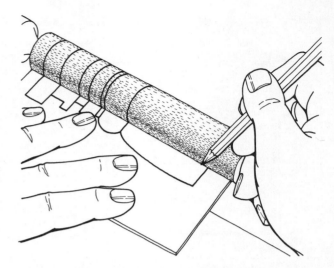

Illus. 105. Before you finish cutting the template cardboard, mark the position of the various necks and hollows on the 1"-diameter cylinder.

Now, take the tool of your choice and gradually waste the hollows, using the pilot cuts and a cardboard template as a guide. Don't try to turn off the waste in one great hurried thrust; it's much better to ease it out with a series of little-by-little, side-to-side sweeps of the tool. Working from left to right, try to establish the size and diameter of the base disc, the shape of the hat, the length and diameter of the head-to-hat spigot, the shape of the head, the neck, the smooth curve of the bosom, the waist, and the gentle sweep of the dress.

Once you have achieved all the convex and concave curves and all the sharp angles that are involved in making up the form, take the wood to a good sanded finish. Be very careful not to overdo the sanding and thus blur all the beautifully crisp angles. With a piece of sandpaper, try to delicately remove only the burrs and rough areas. Finally, look over the workpiece, just to make sure that everything is correct, and then remove it from the lathe.

Carving, Whittling, and Drilling

When you have taken the workpiece off the lathe and established the exact position of the two cut points, meaning the lines between the hat and the base, and the hat and the head spigot, secure the straight saw in the vise so that the teeth are uppermost and then run the workpiece carefully back and forth across the teeth, cutting it down into its three parts.

Now, take the drill and bit, secure the hat brimside up in the jaws of a muffled vise, and then, noting the size of the head spigot, work a suitable hole.

When this is done, refer back to Illus. 102 and note the length and diameter of the two stick legs; then drill two holes in the base and the underside of the skirt accordingly.

Now, take two scraps of wood and a sharp knife and whittle the two little flat arms. Don't try to work details, such as fingers; just stay within the naïve imagery and cut in the line of the cuff, the curve of the elbow, and the roundness of the shoulder. When you have whittled the arms, establish the attachment points on both the arms and the body, and then drill the holes, as shown in Illus. 106.

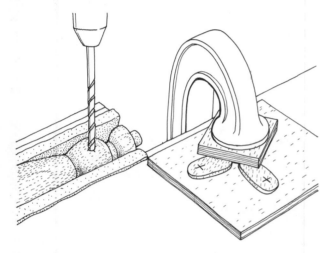

Illus. 106. Secure the turning in the vise, and the arms with a clamp. Then drill the holes for the attachments.

When you reach this stage, have a dry fitting; that is, stand Mrs. Noah on her two stick legs, pop her hat on her head spigot, peg-attach her arms, and generally check her over for size and fit. If the legs are too long, the hat too tight, the arms not quite right, or there is any other problem, take a knife and trim the workpiece so that you achieve a good fit.

When this has been done, refer back to Illus. 102 once more to see how Mrs. Noah's back needs to be carved, and then use the knife to slice away the waste. Hold the figure so that the skirt end is nearest you, and working from the waist to the neck, make two or three controlled cuts. Again, don't try for carefully modelled realism; just slice away the wood from the waistline to the neck so that the figure appears to have a straight flat back and a rounded bosom.

Finally, make a little nick with the knife at the nose position, and then cut, carve, and dry-fit the figure's characteristic triangular chip nose.

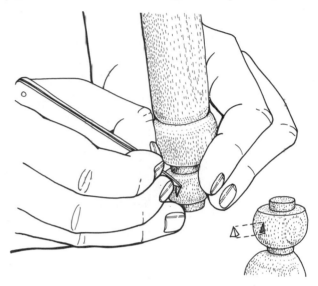

Illus. 107. Use a sharply pointed knife to cut the little chip nose.

Putting the Parts Together

Clear the workbench and set out all the parts of the figure. You should have ten parts in all: the main skittle turning, the hat, two stick legs, the base, two flat arms, two arm pegs, and the nose.

Now, starting from the base and working up, dab glue into the two base holes and push home the two little stick legs. Next, glue the two holes in the underside of the skirt and set the main body on the two legs. Make sure that the figure stands upright, and then glue, fit, and peg-attach the arms on the body. Finally, glue the hat on the head and the little wedge nose in the slot (Illus. 108).

Now, stand Mrs. Noah on a dais and check her over. Are the arms right? Is the nose straight and placed in the correct direction? Is the main body standing upright on the stick legs? Generally run a critical eye over your little creation and then make any necessary modifications.

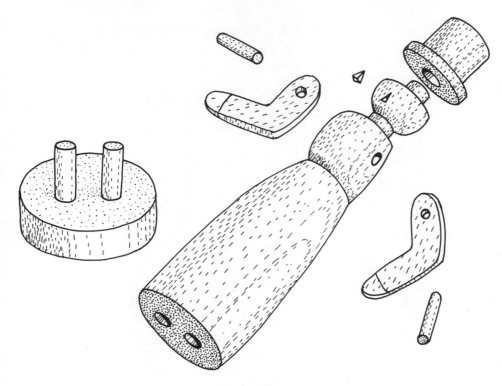

Illus. 108. Dab glue into the
holes, and then fit and
attach the various parts.

Illus. 109. Painting stages.
Left: Paint most of the
workpiece yellow. Middle:
Paint the hat red, the dress
stripes green, and the face
white. Right: Paint the
hatband, the eyes, and the
hair black.

102

Painting and Finishing

When the glue has dried, place Mrs. Noah back up on the dais and set out your acrylic paints, brushes, paint containers, and cloths.

Start by wiping the figure over with a damp cloth to make sure that it is free from dust. Then use a broad brush to apply a primer and a white base coat. Be sure to work the paint into all the little angles under the arms and the hat. If you are making other figures, repeat this process with the next figure to be painted.

After about half an hour, when the base white coat is dry, apply a single smooth coat of your main ground color. If you are following our design, you'll be painting everything, bar the head and the hat, a good, rich primary yellow. Wait a short time for the paint to dry, and then paint the hat, the neck band, and the two outer stripes on the skirt a bright red; highlight the front of the skirt with a stripe of green; and finally paint the eyes and the hair black (Illus. 109).

When the paint is completely dry, give the figure a generous coat of gloss varnish and then put it to one side to dry out.

Troubleshooting and Possible Modifications

• Although we have designed the figure so that the hat fits on a head spigot, there's no reason why you shouldn't work the hat, head, and body as a single turning.

• If you want the figure to have pivotal arms, meaning arms that move, drill right through the body, and use a loosely fitting body dowel and glue the ends of the dowel in the arm holes.

• If you want to work a batch of figures, set a much longer piece of wood in the lathe—say, a piece about 36" long—and turn off six figures at a time.

• By slightly modifying the legs so that they are touching side by side, it is possible to turn off the hat, head, body, legs, and base from the same piece of wood.

Project 3
Making an Ostrich in the Erzgebirge Tradition

Design, Structure, and Technique Considerations

With its amazing two-toed feet, totally bald head, black eyes, long, sweeping eyelashes, and complete inability to fly, our good friend *Struthio camelus* has just got to be the strangest of all the Ark animals.

It may not be the most graceful of creatures, but when it comes to plumage, running, and appetite, the ostrich is hard to beat. For instance, ostrich feathers are so amazingly beautiful that ladies of fashion once ornamented their dresses with them, and, so, many ostrich farms were set up to meet this need. As for running, did you know that the ostrich is the fastest creature on two legs and can reach speeds in excess of 40 miles an hour? And, of course, the ostrich's capacious appetite is legendary. Ostriches normally eat small birds, berries, insects, grass, and the like, and often supplement their diets with bits of stone, bone, and twigs. But it is on record that one ostrich at the London Zoo was found to have swallowed a yard of string, two 4-inch nails, a pencil, a block of wood, three gloves, a metal staple, a handful of small change, several keys, a couple of screws, a gold necklace, and quite a few other odds and ends besides. It's enough to say that the ostrich is a wondrous beast, and this is why it has always been a favorite with Ark builders.

However, the ostrich is not the easiest animal to make; in fact, in the context of this book, it is one of the most difficult. This is because the ostrich has long legs and a long neck springing out from a comparatively small body, so that it is difficult to carve the form from a single piece of wood and still get a strong grain-related structure. Thus, it's best to build up this animal from four separate pieces of wood—a pear-shaped piece for the body, two longish pieces for the legs, and a long S-shaped piece for the head and neck.

Take a look at Illus. 112 and see how the neck and the legs need to be worked so that the grain of the wood will run most efficiently through the carving. Since the legs would be too weak if they were carved across the grain, they must be worked so that the grain runs up and down from the body to the toes.

Study all the accompanying drawings, take a look at carved Ark animals in toy shops and museums, and, if at all possible, visit a zoo and try to see an ostrich in the flesh. Finally, draw your designs accordingly.

Illus. 110. Project picture. The ostrich is about 4" high, from the top of the base to the top of the head.

Tools and Materials

For this project you need:
- a quantity of easy-to-carve wood, such as lime—a piece of 1½" X 2" and 2½" long for the body, a piece 1" X 1" and 2½" long for the head and neck, a piece 1" X 1" and 2" long for one leg, a piece 1½" X 1" and 2" long for the other leg, and finally a piece 3" X 2" and ¼" thick for the base;
- Plasticine;
- about 24" of easy-to-bend coat-hanger wire;
- a roll of thin fuse-type wire;
- a pair of pliers;
- a small hammer;
- a roll of masking tape;
- a small slab of rough wood;
- half a dozen small fencing staples;
- a pair of callipers;
- a measure;
- a modelling tool—the type used for clay sculpture;
- a coping saw;
- a selection of whittling knives, such as a small penknife, a broad-bladed knife, and a scalpel;
- a pencil and a pad of work-out paper;
- tracing paper;
- a pack of graded sandpapers;
- a small riffler file;
- a two-tube, fast-setting resin glue;

Illus. 111. Inspirational drawing. If you're looking for other flightless birds, how about trying one of these? Top left: Sub-Antarctic jackass penguin. Top right: Australian emu. Middle left: New Zealand kiwi. Bottom left: New Guinean and Australian cassowary. Bottom right: Antarctic Adélie penguin.

- wood primer;
- a selection of acrylic paints, including white, brown, blue-black, and yellow;
- varnish;
- a selection of brushes; and
- the use of a workbench and a vise.

Making a Model

First, pin up your working drawings and any photographs you may have collected, and set out the two types of wire, the pliers, the slab of rough wood, the staples, the hammer, and the Plasticine.

Now, with one eye on the drawings, clip off two

lengths of coat-hanger wire—one piece at about 8" and the other at about 3". Use the staples to attach the wire to the wood, as shown in Illus. 113, and then bend, shape, and bind the wire into an armature. This armature will serve as a framework for your model. See how, in Illus. 113, the long piece of wire runs up one leg and right through to the head, whereas the other piece runs up one leg and is tied at the body into the first leg. Make the wire-to-wire joint secure by binding it with fuse wire and covering it with a strip of masking tape.

Work the Plasticine for a moment or two until it is soft, and then quickly wrap it around the wire frame. At this point don't bother too much with any elaborate modelling; just try to quickly build up the body mass. Once you have covered all the wire and built out the body, and you are sure that all the Plasticine is going to stay put, then you can start to model the details. Fill out the broad flat body and rudimentary wings; fatten up the knees and upper legs; and build the peculiar eye ridges, the long flat beak, and all the other characteristic features. Generally, spend some time modelling out and cutting back until you have a suitable form for an ostrich.

Cutting Out the Blanks

Once you have made a good model, set it near your working drawings, clear away the scraps of Plasticine, and set out all your tools and materials.

Now, trace the four profiles from your working drawings—meaning the side views of the head and neck, the body, and the two legs—and, with a pencil, press-transfer the lines of the tracings through to the side faces of the correct pieces of wood. Make sure that the transferred lines are bold, check to be sure that the drawn profiles relate correctly to the run of the grain, shade in the profiles, and then use the coping saw to cut away the waste (Illus. 114).

Now, using your model as a guide, take a series of calliper readings and mark out on the sawn blanks

On the opposite page: Illus. 112. Working-drawing grid. The scale is four grid squares to 1". Note the shape of the wire-model armature, and how the various blocks need to be set in relationship to the run of their grain and to the total form.

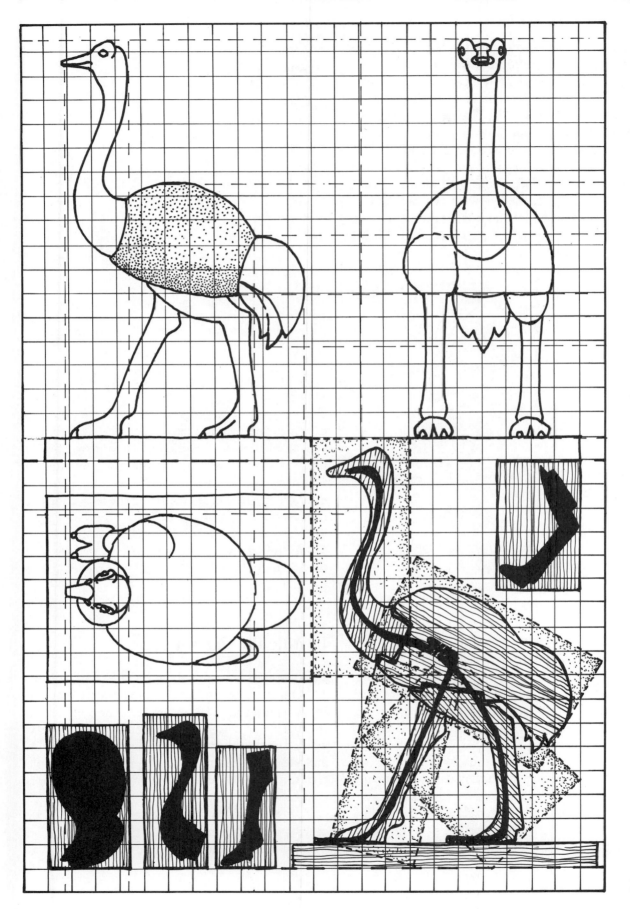

107

the front, top, and bottom profiles. When you have mapped out a series of dotted calliper readings on the sawn faces of the four flat-faced blanks, connect the dots with a pencil line, and again shade in the areas that need to be wasted. Compare the partially worked forms with your drawings and your model, making sure that you've got them right, and then use the coping saw to clear away the waste. Continue taking calliper readings from your drawings and model, drawing in revised views, and clearing away the increasingly smaller and smaller pieces of waste until you have worked the four pieces of wood down to their squared forms.

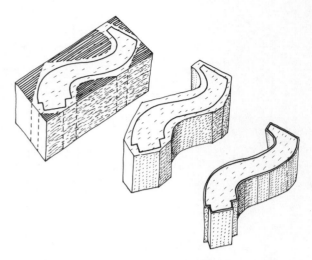

Illus. 114. With a pencil, press-transfer the side view through to the working face of the wood, and then use a coping saw to clear away the waste. (The stages are shown from top to bottom.)

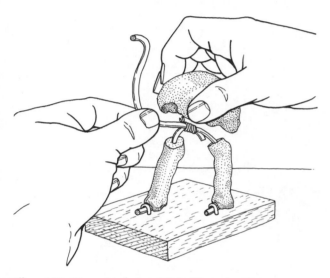

Illus. 113. To make the model, build up the Plasticine on the wire armature.

Whittling

Take the ostrich body in one hand and the broad knife in the other, note any peculiarities in the run of the grain, and then begin paring and modelling. Make a stop cut around the wood at the point where the tail appears to be growing out of the body; then, working with a series of careful, well-considered and -controlled thumb-paring cuts, whittle in from both ends of the wood. In other words, by turn, whittle in from the tail and the neck ends of the wood and use the stop cut as a knife check, or block. As you carve and shape the wood, and get closer to the desired form, keep the wood moving and work with smaller and smaller strokes. And, so, you'll be working the

neck and head, as well as the two legs, simply shaving and paring away at the wood, all the while checking off your progress against your working drawings and your model.

At this stage, don't work the four forms to a highly finished state; just establish the main features by removing all the sawn faces and rough angles. For example, when you are whittling the legs, chop out the overall shape of the two toes, the large bony knees, and the thicker upper leg, but don't cut in the surface texture and be certain to stop well short of the top end of the leg. Work all four pieces in like manner.

Putting the Parts Together

Before you go any further, take a close look at Illus. 115 and see how the legs and the neck are tenoned into a body mortise. For example, at the point where the neck joins the body, the end of the neck is worked so that there is a shoulder spigot, or tenon, and the body is mortised. Or, to put it in very simple terms, a hole is made in the body, and the neck is pushed into it.

The best way to start working on a joint is by carving a flat face on the body and cutting a hole. The hole can be round, square, triangular, or slot-

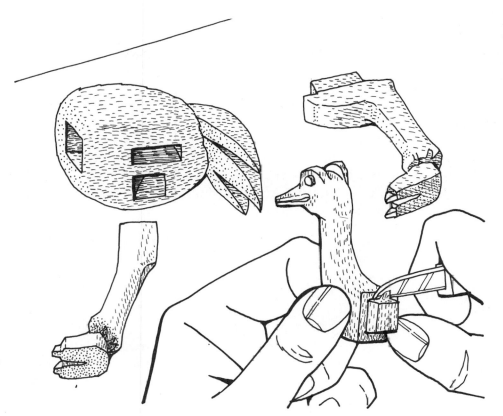

Illus. 115. Once you have roughed out the main forms, and cut and fit the mortise-and-tenon joints, attach the parts with resin glue.

like; the shape doesn't matter, as long as it corresponds to the piece that is to be fitted. You might want to cut a round hole for the neck that is about ³/₈" in diameter, and leg holes that are about ¹/₄" wide and ³/₄" long. Don't worry too much about the depth of the holes; about ¹/₄" will be fine. When you come to working the spigots on the neck and legs, first use the knife to make a ¹/₈"-deep stop cut around the wood; then slice in from the end of the wood to make a spigot to fit the hole and a square-cut shoulder to lap over the hole and butt up against the body. Be extra careful at this point; don't try to hack away the waste in one great lump, but rather become aware of the run of the grain and then slowly cut the wood back with a number of small, well-considered strokes. When you have cut the spigot to fit the hole, shape the shoulder so that, as the spigot slides home and the two pieces of wood come together, the flat face of the shoulder meets the flat face of the body to make a smooth flush fit.

When you have whittled and fit the neck and the two legs, and the whole workpiece looks right, generously dab all joints with resin glue, and then put the workpiece to one side.

Modelling the Details

When the glue is dry, pick up the workpiece and give it a critical once-over, comparing it with your drawings and model. As likely as not, especially if you are a beginner, the whole piece will look a little disjointed and thrown together. But this won't matter because, if you have worked as described, there should still be plenty of spare surface wood to allow you to carve across the joints with a scalpel so that the entire piece will begin to run together. But, first, take a look at the grain, especially at the joints, and note difficult twists and fragile areas of short grain.

Now, with the workpiece held in one hand or, perhaps, cradled on a cushion on your lap, take the smallest, sharpest knife and the riffler file, and cut in all the details. Try, as you are working, to draw attention away from the joints by creating some part of the textural details across the breaks. For example, you might take the feather pattern down the leg, and you might make some cuts into the body so that the visual breaks occur below the actual joints. When you have worked all the details of the head, neck, legs, and feet, cut in a stylized feather texture over the entire body. Finally, glue the ostrich in place on its base.

Painting and Finishing

When you come to painting, stop and consider how you want your ostrich to look. Are you going to strive for a simple painterly effect that suggests the various areas, the body feathers, the tail, and all the rest? Or, are you going to create a more definite image, highlighting all the small details? Regardless of the style you choose, you'll first need to wipe the wood over with a damp cloth, tidy up your work area, and set out all your painting materials.

Start by applying the primer and base coats, and then, in the 30 minutes, or so, while the paint is drying, refresh your memory by studying your illustrations of ostriches. Note the pinkish brown neck, the huge black eyes, the long, black eyelashes, the way the feathers change color from pink to white to black at the lower end of the neck, the huge white tail feathers, and the brownish, rippled, chickenlike legs.

When the primer and base coats are dry, apply the various top colors. You might want to use a fine-point brush to paint the details, and a dry brush to go over the body with black so that some of the white underneath is revealed, thereby creating a feather effect (Illus. 116). Then you might want to paint the base a yellow-green. Finally, give the entire piece a generous coat of gloss varnish.

Troubleshooting and Possible Modifications

• If you don't like the idea of having the neck and legs spigotted into the body, you can use drilled holes and dowels instead.

• Rather than using separate parts, you can have either the neck or one of the legs worked directly out of the wood of the body.

• You might consider using glue and real feathers instead of paint.

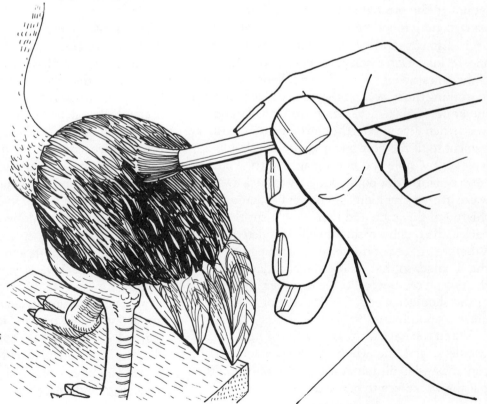

Illus. 116. Once you have whittled and carved the ostrich to a fine finish, and once the coat of base paint is dry, paint the body black; then scuff through the black paint with a dry brush to create a feather effect.

Project 4
Making a Crocodile in the Erzgebirge Tradition

Design, Structure, and Technique Considerations

Who can blame the crocodile when it sheds those fabled hypocritical tears over its prey so that it can lure further victims to their doom. It can't be much fun being hunted down, only to be turned into shoes and handbags. But don't you shed too many tears for the poor old crocodile because, in fact, it spends most of its days just lazing about by the river and basking in the sun, and that can't be too bad. . . . Now, of course, Noah usually kept well clear of "unclean abominations that creep and creepeth upon the belly," but when it came to allotting space in the Ark, we have a hunch he found room for a couple of crocodiles in the bilges. Incidentally, we thought we should also mention that since crocodiles and alligators are so similar, you can make an alligator instead if you want to.

Take a look at the various accompanying drawings and see how this large amphibious reptile has a huge, unfriendly, ragged-toothed mouth, massive jaws, a long lashing tail, and a squishy body that spreads out on the sides and is almost completely covered with horny scales. Note, in Illus. 119, how the carving is built up from five primary parts: the main nose-to-tail body and the four legs. See how the legs are dowel-attached onto the sides of the body and how the whole beast flattens out at the base; study the jaws, the teeth, the spiny ridge that runs down the back, and generally familiarize yourself with all the creepy leviathan characteristics that make the crocodile so endearing. Of course, if you want to redesign the croc so that it is longer or wider, has a closed mouth, is entirely cut from a single piece of wood, or whatever, then now is the time to consider such modifications. If you are wondering why, even though the grain runs longitudinally through the whole beast, we have made the croc from five pieces of wood rather than, say, from one large piece, the answer is simple enough. It's best to carve the main, curvy nose-to-tail form with a series of swift and easy strokes through the wood. If the workpiece had to be carved all-in-one, then the jutting-out legs would interrupt the sweep of the knife. It is much easier to carve the legs separately and attach them later. However, it's always a good idea to consider design and technique modifications because you just might hit upon a new angle or better approach.

In the course of your preparations for this project, visit toy museums, go to see crocs and alligators in

Illus. 117. Project picture. The crocodile is about 6" long from snout to tail. Note how the chip-carved horny scales are largest on the head end of the back, and how they get smaller as they near the tail and the legs.

zoos and local pet shops, collect photographs and magazine clips, and make a series of sketches and studies. Then take a piece of Plasticine and make a model.

Tools and Materials

For this project you need:

- a quantity of easy-to-carve wood—a piece 1" X 1" and 6" long for the body, two pieces ¾" X ½" and 1 ¼" long for the back legs, and two pieces ½" X ½" and 1 ¼" long for the front legs;
- about 2" of ⅛" dowel—or you can use off cuts and make your own;
- a coping saw with a pack of spare blades;
- a couple of whittling knives;
- a small hand drill with a ⅛" drill bit;
- a small, long-pointed riffler file;
- a round-section rasp;
- pencils and a pad of work-out paper;
- a pack of graded sandpapers;
- a selection of acrylic paints;
- primer and varnish;
- a selection of brushes;
- a small piece of sponge;

- PVA wood glue; and
- the use of a workbench and vise.

Marking Out Your Design and Doing the Initial Steps

Arrange your work area so that all the drawings and photographs are in view, and make sure that the tools are in good condition and within reach. Spend some time drawing to size the side views of the body and the legs; then make a tracing, and with a pencil, press-transfer the lines of the design through to the working side faces of your pieces of carefully selected wood. First, checking to make sure that the lower jaw isn't curving up too far at the front and thus causing an area of short grain, take a soft pencil and shade in all the areas around the profile that need to be cut away.

When you have done this with all five profiles, secure the wood in the vise, a piece at a time, and begin cutting away the waste. Although we use a coping saw, you can also use a small bow saw, a pad saw, a straight saw and a rasp, or even a drawknife, as long as you manage to clear away the waste and end up with good, clean-cut profile blanks. As you are working, follow the drawn lines as closely as possible, but try to cut on the waste side so that there is about ⅛" of spare wood between your line of cut and the pencil line. When you work around the lower jaw, be careful not to force the saw and thus split the wood.

Cutting the Blanks

When you have worked the side-view cutouts, place them on the workbench so that you see them all top-on, and then begin to draw the top views on the wood. Of course, when you are working on sawn, undulating faces, it's much more difficult to visualize the views. But still do your best to clearly pencil

Illus. 118. Inspirational drawing. If you want to try your hand at another lizard type of creature, how about one of the following? Top: South American iguana. Second from top: African spiny-tailed agamid. Second from bottom: Nile monitor. Bottom: three-horned chameleon.

in the views and the areas of waste that need to be cut away.

Having looked at Illus. 119 and noted the beautiful curve of the tail and the way the legs butt up against the croc's belly, set the wood in the vise and start cutting away the waste accordingly. Working the legs is fairly straightforward, as long as you make sure that you mirror-image the cutouts so that you have left and right legs (Illus. 120); but when you come to working the body, then you will have to watch out for the grain. You will have to be especially careful when you are cutting around the tail so that you don't split the wood in the weak areas of short grain that run across the curves. Again, don't cut too near your drawn lines; just try to clear them by about the thickness of the saw blade. Work all five pieces in this manner.

When this is done, set the blanks out on the workbench so that you can see them top-on. Label the legs *left front, left back,* and so on, and generally check your progress against Illus. 119 and 120. Then identify and label the leg-to-body faces of all four legs and the points on the sides of the body where they fit.

Whittling the Body

Clear away the waste and the large bench tools. You should be comfortably seated, with the croc's body in one hand and a fairly large, sharp knife in the other. Having first studied the run of the grain, start to cut away the rough with a series of strokes that are directed away from you. As you whittle, tuck your elbows into your sides, and control the distance of your strokes by holding your wrists tight against your body (Illus. 121). As you work, hold the croc by its head and carve it from its belly to its tail; then turn it around so that you are holding it by its tail, and carve it from its belly to its snout. At this stage, don't try to carve any details or textures; just try to create a body that is smooth and curved, with a flat base—sort of like a curvy Cornish pasty, or turnover, with one sharp end. In fact, as with a Cornish pasty, the

On the following page: Illus. 119. Working drawing. The scale is four grid squares to 1″. See how the legs are carved to fit, and how they are attached with pegs.

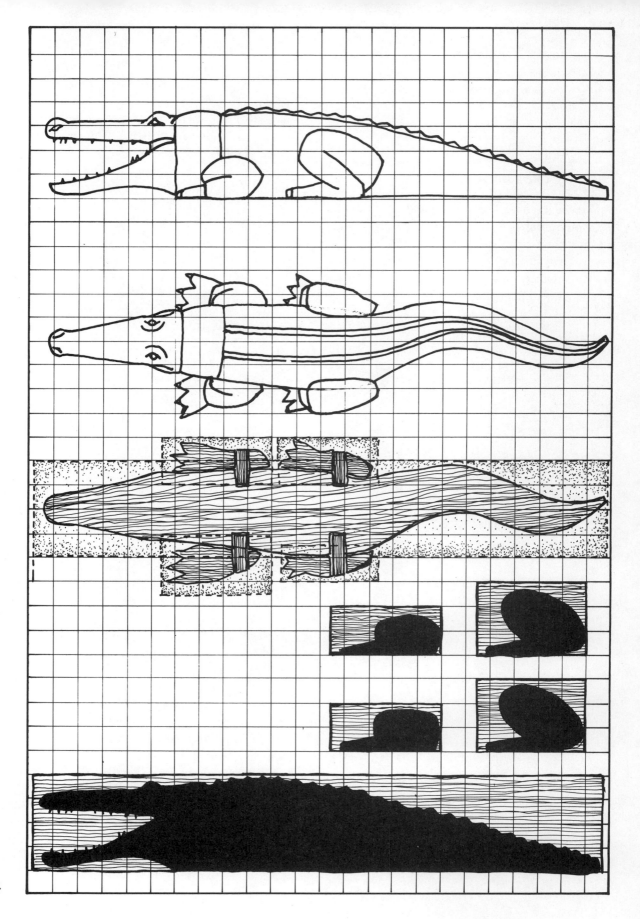

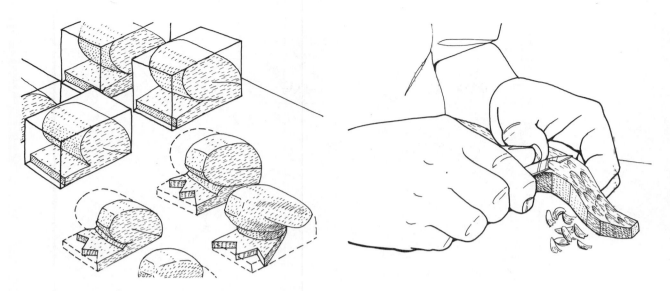

Illus. 120 (left). When you cut the blanks, make sure that you correctly "mirror-image" the cutouts so that you get left and right legs. Illus. 121 (right). As you whittle, control the knife strokes by tucking your elbows into your sides and by holding your wrists tight against your body.

croc not only needs to have a flat base and nicely rounded, bulging sides, but it also needs to have a spiny sharp-ridged back.

When you have cleared away the rough with a series of broad strokes directed away from yourself, then change your approach and start to whittle with a tight thumb-paring action towards yourself. You can still hold the croc by its head, but this time have its tail pointing towards yourself and pare towards yourself from its belly to its tail.

Try, as you are whittling, to run the knife from high wood to low. For example, when you are cutting a concave curve, then you should work in from both sides so that the blade runs from high ground and finishes up in the dip, and when you are working a convex curve, you should run the knife from the high ground and work out and down. It's all simple enough, as long as you are wary about cutting into end grain. Then again, it can be somewhat tricky when you come to carving the inside of the lower jaw. With the rule of thumb about cutting into end grain in mind, when you start to carve inside the mouth try to either work the knife from the back of the throat out towards the snout, or use the smallest, sharpest scalpel and work at a sharp angle across the grain. It's best to work with a fine-bladed scalpel; then, if by chance, the blade does run into the grain, the blade will snap off rather than the croc's entire lower jaw.

Fitting the Legs

When the body and the legs are more or less finished, set them out on your work surface and see how they all fit in relationship to each other. Now, refer back to Illus. 119 and see how the legs need to fit snuggly against the sides of the croc's body. You can flatten off both the body and the legs so that they can come together in a good fit; or, better still, you can shape the inside faces of the legs so that they follow and fit the curves of the body.

Use the rasp and the riffler file to hollow-curve the leg-to-body faces of all four legs. When this is done, bring the croc's legs against its body and strap them in place with masking tape. When you have checked the position and fit, making sure that you haven't fitted the legs back-to-front or the wrong way around, take the hand drill and the ⅛" bit, and bore holes through the legs and into the body (Illus. 122). Remove the masking tape, cut four dowels, and then glue the legs to the body. Finally, trim off the ends of the dowels with a scalpel.

Finishing and Painting

Once the glue is dry comes the delightful task of texturing the scales. Refer back to Illus. 117 and see how the scales vary in size and shape depending upon where they appear on the crocodile.

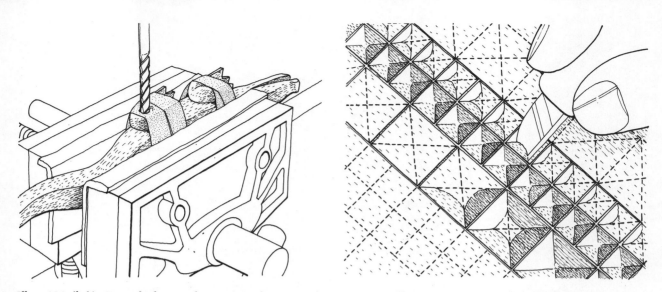

Illus. 122 (left). Tape the legs in place, secure the croc in the jaws of a muffled vise, and then drill the peg holes. Illus. 123 (right). To make the scales, mark out the square grid and cut in the shape of the squares; then slice down from the center of the squares to create the chip-carved pyramid forms.

Before you start, it would be a good idea to take a scrap of waste wood and do some trial carving. It's really somewhat similar to chip carving in that the small pyramidlike scales are each systematically worked with half a dozen, or so, mechanical strokes. You first make four cuts to establish the squarish perimeter of a scale; then you work out from the center of the square, carving down into the perimeter stop cuts (Illus. 123).

Make four center-to-side cuts for each scale. If you vary the size and depth of the scales, the overall effect can be quite exciting.

Carve all the small details around the eyes, inside the mouth, and so on. Then go over the entire workpiece with a scalpel, tidying up all the creases and crannies, so that it ends up looking crisp and clean.

Now, clean up your work area, making sure that it is free from dust and debris, and set out the brushes, the scrap of sponge, and the acrylic paints.

First, wipe the croc over with a damp cloth and then, remembering to let the paint dry out between coats, apply the primer and the undercoat. Next,

apply a dark-green ground color. When the ground color is dry, dip the sponge in slightly yellowish green paint and dab it on the croc's top side. By painting the surface this way, the scales will appear to be in high relief. Then use a fine-point brush to highlight the details of the eyes and mouth. Finally, give the entire workpiece a couple of coats of varnish.

Troubleshooting and Possible Modifications

• You might prefer to work a very simplified, smooth-profiled, low-relief crocodile, in which case the whole beast can be cut from a single piece of wood.

• If you want to mount the crocodile on a base, then you can leave out the leg-strengthening dowels.

• You can redesign the project and use loose-fitting dowels through the body. Such a modification would result in a crocodile that looks like it is walking when it's lifted and moved from side to side.

Project 5
Making a Peacock in the Erzgebirge Tradition

Design, Structure, and Technique Considerations

By all accounts, King Solomon was amazingly rich: He had four thousand horses, tons of gold, a throne made from ivory and gold, and a great friend in the queen of Sheba, who delighted in giving him presents of precious stones. His very name now conjures

Illus. 124. Project picture. The peacock measures about 6" from the tip of the head crest to the end of the tail.

up pictures of wealth and extravagance. Every three years or so, ships from Ceylon not only brought Solomon even more gold, but, also, beautiful peacocks. It is unknown whether he wanted these birds to strut around his garden for ornamentation, or to be served up at dinner as the main course. But we do know that peacocks have always been status symbols; so, if you have a grand house and a golden chariot, then you really do need a pride of peacocks to round out the picture. Not only do peacocks bring to mind images of ostentation, pride, and vanity, but they were once worshipped as gods, feared because of their evil-eye plumage, eaten by early Christians for their everlasting-life qualities, and thought by Mohammedans to be guardians of paradise. Suffice it to say that if you want to make a full set of Ark animals, then this magnificent bird can't be left out.

Take a look at Illus. 124 and 125 and see how the peacock's tail, or train, makes up at least half of the bird's length. Note the "eye" markings on the tail, the body plumage, and the crownlike head crest. See how, at a grid scale of four squares to 1", our bird measures about 6" from crest to tail. Although this project shows the tail in it train state, you can alter the design so that the feathers fan out in a more exciting display.

As with all the other animal-making projects,

117

Illus. 125. Inspirational drawing. Birds are beautiful! Make some sketches of your own, or perhaps try one of these. Top left: European mute swan. Top right: European heron. Middle right: head detail of a European spoonbill. Middle left: European white stork. Bottom left: head detail of a European pelican. Bottom right: European capercaillie.

Be sure to look over all the drawings accompanying the project and note all the tool and technique problems involved in fitting the parts together. Then draw the various views to size. Finally, as with the ostrich project, make a Plasticine and wire model.

Tools and Materials

For this project you need:
- five pieces of lime—a piece about 1¼" X 1" and 2" long for the body, two pieces 1" X 1" X 1" for the feet, a piece 1" X ½" X 1" for the head and neck, a piece about ½" X 2" and 2½" long for the tail, and a piece of ¼"-thick wood for the base;
- a coping saw;
- a small straight saw;
- a couple of small whittling knives;
- a round-section Surform rasp;
- a small hand drill with two drill bits, one at ⅛" and the other at ¼";
- a pack of graded sandpapers;
- pencils and a pad of work-out paper;
- primer and undercoat;
- a selection of acrylic paints, in orange, iridescent blue, green, yellow, purple, and black;
- varnish;
- a quantity of Plasticine;
- about 12" of thin coat-hanger wire;
- a small amount of thin binding wire;
- a selection of brushes;
- PVA wood glue; and
- the use of a workbench and vise.

Cutting the Profile Blanks

When you have drawn your designs and made your model, note how the run of the wood grain needs to correspond to the forms. For example, the wood grain should run along the length of the tail, up the neck, and up the legs. Now, take tracings from your profile views. When this is done, take a pencil and

you can't really begin to carve the project until you are familiar with its form. Certainly, you may think that you know exactly what, say, a dog, cat, cow, or crocodile looks like, but you probably only have in mind a rather generalized image. And so it is with a peacock; you may know it has a splendid tail and a delicate crest, but how certain are you really about the shape and color of all the parts in between? So, before you start, spend some time getting to know your subject. Look at peacocks in picture books and search them out at zoos and animal parks. Make sketches, collect photographs, and study the "eye" feathers.

On the opposite page: Illus. 126. Working drawing. Top: The scale is about four grid squares to 1". Note how the bird is made up from five parts. Also, see how, prior to carving, you need to build a Plasticine model around a wire armature.

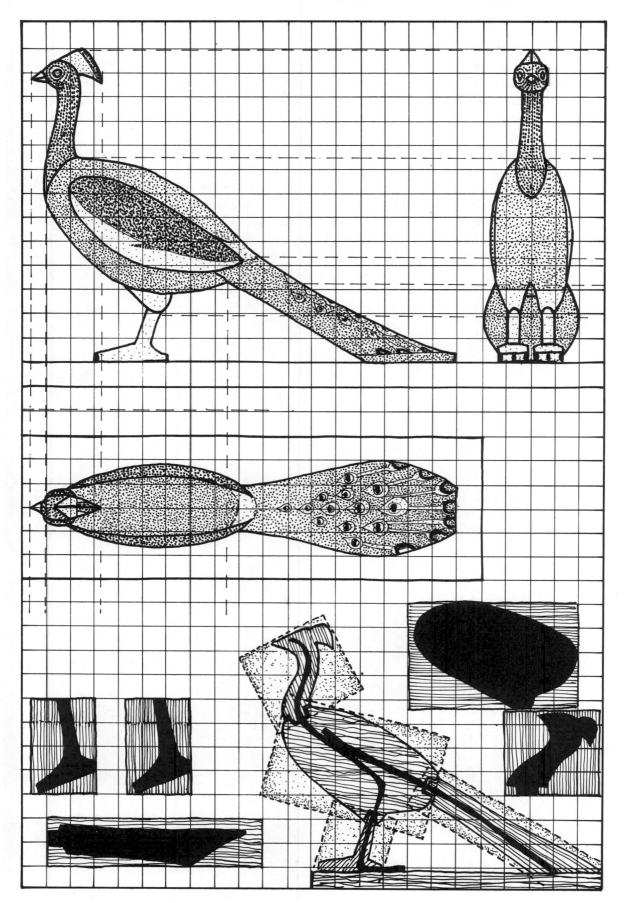

119

press-transfer the traced lines through the side faces of the wood. It's important for the transferred lines and the drawn forms to be well established. So make a point of shading in the areas of waste that need to be cut away.

Now, a piece at a time, set the wood in the vise and use one of your saws to clear away the waste (Illus. 127). You might use the coping saw for cutting out the slender head and the delicate feet, and the straight saw for the thicker-sectioned body and tail. When you have roughed out the two bulkier shapes, meaning the body and the tail, use the tube rasp to clean up the profile views so that they run smoothly and uniformly through the thickness of the wood. You should now have five cleanly worked profile blanks—the head, the body, the tail, and the two legs.

Rounding the Forms

Firsts, set the five pieces of wood out so that they correspond to each other and can be viewed "plan"-on. Now, go back to your working drawings, trace off the "plan" views, and then, bearing in mind the differences between the views as drawn on paper and those seen on the wood, use the tracings to draw in the top profiles (Illus. 128). The main-body form is straightforward enough in that the side and top views are both, more or less, egg shaped, but the

other parts are a little more complicated. For example, the tail, as seen side-on, appears to be a thin strip, whereas, in plan view, it looks more like a long half-closed fan. If you have any doubts as to how a particular piece of wood ought to look, refer back to your model, and, if necessary, take a block of Plasticine through the various carving stages. When you have sketched the modified plan views out on the wood, identify the profile outline and use one of the saws to cut away the waste.

When this is done, put the large tools to one side, clear away the offcuts, and then prepare to work with the knives. The body and the tail are easy enough to carve—all you do is trim off the corners and you are halfway finished—but the smaller shapes are more difficult. For instance, when you come to carving the head front-on, then not only do you need to sharpen the wood to form the beak, but you also need to cut away the waste at both sides of the top of the head so as to achieve the characteristically narrow-based, broad-topped wedge shape of the crest. And when you come to carving the two foot-and-leg pieces, you'll see that the side, or profile, views are straightforward since they are really no more than upside-down T-shapes that run through the thickness of the wood, but the front views are more complicated. Although front-on the foot uses the full width of the wood, it is necessary for you to cut away a strip from both sides of the central leg

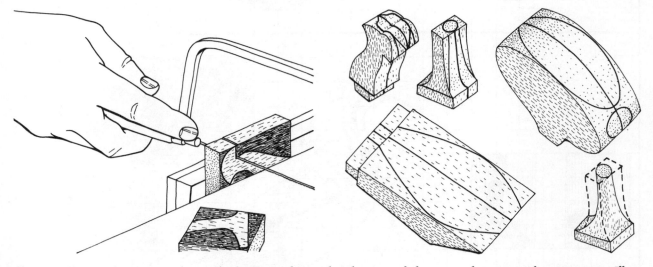

Illus. 127 (left). When you cut the profile blanks, set the wood in the vise and clear away the waste with a coping saw. Illus. 128 (right). Once you have cut away the waste as seen in the side views, then draw in the forms and identify the waste from the top views.

120

column. You should finish up with two upside-down, square-headed T-shapes, one for each foot (refer back to the details in Illus. 126).

Putting the Parts Together

Once you have rounded off the sawn blanks and made five pieces with peacock characteristics, then comes the time to put it all together. Refer back to Illus. 126 and also study your model, and see how the legs, head, and tail are jointed into the body. Especially note the angles at which the additions spring out from the central body.

Now, take the hand drill and the ⅛" drill bit, mark the position of the two legs on the underside of the body, and get ready to drill the two leg holes, or mortises. You should support the body piece in the jaws of a rag-muffled vise, and spend some time getting the angle of the holes just right. Then drill into the wood to a depth of about ⅛".

Now, a piece at a time, take the two feet and use a knife to whittle the leg stumps to a ⅛" taper, and then set the legs in the leg holes.

When you are sure that both legs are set at the same angle and depth, move on to fitting the tail. Drill a ¼"-diameter hole and taper the tail stump to a good fit and angle. Continue in this manner with the head.

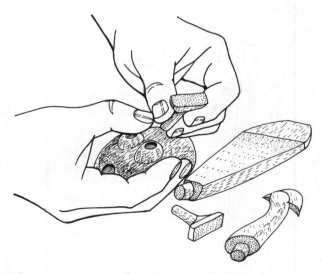

Illus. 129. To put it all together, take the roughed-out pieces, whittle their stumps to fit the mortise holes, and then glue them in.

When you have fitted all the parts (the legs, head, and tail) and when you are happy with the overall shape and posture of the peacock, remove, glue, and refit the additions (Illus. 129). Finally, when you have made sure that the peacock is standing upright, glue it on its base and then put it to one side for about 24 hours.

Modelling

When the glue is dry, set the peacock out on the workbench and spend some time organizing your work area and sharpening all your knives. Then refresh your eye by looking at your model and all your drawings and photographs. Study the form and try to analyze those characteristics that identify it as a peacock. The elephant is characterized by its trunk and size, the ostrich by its naked neck and long legs, and the crocodile by its jaws and teeth. With the peacock, is it its tail, crest, or coloring—or perhaps the sum total of these details? Study the peacock and try to get a firm grasp of its form, detailing, texture, and color.

Now, with the workpiece in one hand and the knife in the other, note the run of the wood grain, and then start to whittle away at the joints. As with the ostrich, try to reduce the bulk of the wood so that the form runs in a smooth convincing line across the various jointed divides. For example, when you are working on the neck, simply forget about the fact that at that point two different pieces of wood come together; just cut away the rough so as to continue the curved lines of the neck smoothly across the joint and down into the body.

Once you have cleaned up the form, take a scalpel or a fine-bladed penknife and start to cut in the details. Slide the blade down and around the curve of the neck; sharpen up the angle where the crest springs out of the head; line in the fine detailing around the beak and eyes; and work the fan-shaped sweep of the tail. Move the blade backwards and forward over the wood, all the while getting closer and closer to the desired form. Work and rework the carving, removing smaller and yet smaller skims, or scoops, of wood. Work towards creating a crisp, clean, slightly dappled surface. Finally, clean up the base with the sandpaper.

Painting and Finishing

Start by clearing away the bench clutter, setting out the paints and brushes, and making sure that your work area is clean and free from dust. Now, remembering to let the paint dry off between coats, swiftly apply the primer and the undercoat.

Then spend some time mixing your range of colors. You need an iridescent blue for the neck, breast, and "eye spots"; a shimmering blue-green for the tail; a brilliant orange for the wing feathers; a small amount of white for around the eyes; a touch of vivid yellow for the beak, crest, and "eye spots"; and, lastly, just a dab or two of blue-black for the eyes, crest, feet, and feather tips. Start with the head, work down towards the tail, and finish up with the "eye spots." Blend the main-body colors into each other; and when you come to painting the "eye spots," run several colors into each other. For ex-

ample, dab on a spot of yellow, and follow it up with a dab of orange, a dab of light blue, and a dab of dark blue. Finally, paint the base green (Illus. 130). Then, when all the paint is dry, apply a couple of coats of gloss varnish.

Troubleshooting and Possible Modifications

- You can modify the design and make the body and the tail all carved from a single piece of wood.
- Rather than setting down the tail in a train, you can have it displayed as a fan.
- When you choose your acrylic paints, go for the iridescent, pearl, or metallic colors.
- Although we have set the peacock on a base in this project, you can modify the design and have the bird standing on its own two feet.

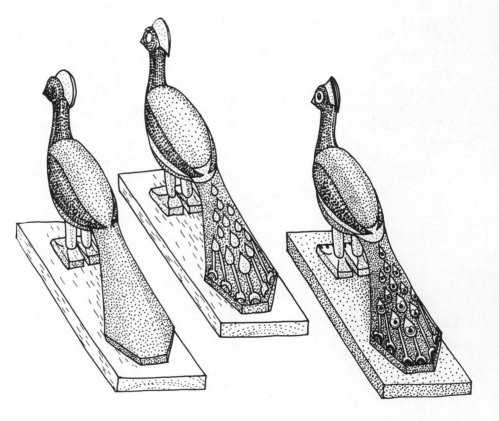

Illus. 130. Painting order, from left to right: First, paint the large background areas blue, green, and yellow; next, paint the feather patterns on the wing and tail, and highlight the "eyes" on the feathers with white; then, paint the details dark blue and the base green.

4
THE CREMER ARK

The Cremer Ark (Illus. 131, and Illus. 4 on page D in the color section) is named after Cremer's, the most famous toy shop in Victorian London. Made in Saxony in the early nineteenth century, this type of Ark is not only beautifully put together and wonderfully stencilled and painted, but it's absolutely jampacked with as many as 300 turned and carved animals.

Most Cremer Arks have a stencilled dove motif on the roof, a stencilled and painted pattern running just under the eaves, stencilled windows, and various stencilled brick and tile motifs on the walls and the roof.

As for the 150, or so, pairs of animals, the Cremer Ark has everything from elephants, pigs, and giraffes to spiders, ladybirds, and beetles, and they are all roughed out on the lathe. The process is beautifully simple—first, by means of templates, various animal-section rings are turned on the lathe, and then they are chopped into slices, carved, and painted. Certainly, cutting and working the animals this way does result in some of the larger four-legged animals looking a bit similar, but traditional turners seemed to be happy turning off, say, a basic horselike ring, and then modifying the slices to create other animals. For example, with some imaginative carving and the addition of such features as horns, antlers, or large ears, horselike slices can easily be made into mules, donkeys, deer, or even large dogs. So, who said Henry Ford invented mass production!

Illus. 131. The Cremer Ark measures 22" to 24" from prow to stern. Note the stencil-decorated roof, windows, and flowers; the prow and stern blocks; the semirounded form; and the sliding-door slots at the prow and stern.

Project 1
Making an Ark in the Cremer Tradition

Design and Structure Considerations

The Cremer Ark is a beauty, not so much because of its size and form, although it is certainly impressive on both counts, but rather because of the way it is decorated. Take a look at the accompanying illustrations, and make a point of searching out a Cremer Ark in a gallery or a museum. When you find a good close-up of such an Ark, study the stencil work and the painting. See how the hard-edged, wavy, tilelike pattern that runs across the roof has been worked with a scalloped stencil, and also note the stencilled windows, the stencilled dove, and the strip of floral pattern that has been stencilled and then painted over. Try to imagine exactly how the stencil cardboard was cut and used. For example, imagine how the blocks of little dark squares within the main window frames must have been made with a stencil plate that printed a 16 square cutout, and how the dove appears to have a stencilled body and how its details look like they were highlighted with a brush. You might also take a magnifying glass to an Ark and study the way the various colors of paint overlap. Note that free brush-worked motifs have a loose, feathered edge while stencilled areas are hard-edged.

Study an Ark and try to imagine how a nineteenth-century Ark builder might have worked out the various building and decorating stages.

As to the actual structure of the Cremer Ark, it follows classic lines by having the usual box hull, the slightly curved prow and stern boards, the house with an end porch, and the long, sliding side-wall door. Take a look at Illus. 133 and see how the hull has been built up from massive plank wood, and note the overall length, height, and breadth of the Ark. Then draw your own design and size specifications; by this we mean, draw views that show the size of the various main areas. Note: Our cutting plan (Illus. 132) is only a diagrammatic generalization; you will need to build a cardboard prototype to finalize measurements.

On the following pages: Illus. 132 (left). The cutting grid. The scale is about one grid square to 2". Illus. 133 (right). Working drawing. Top: The scale is about one grid square to 2". Middle: The scale is about one grid square to 1". Bottom: This is not to scale. Note the through-the-side section, and see how the curves of the prow and stern are achieved by rounding the corner angles.

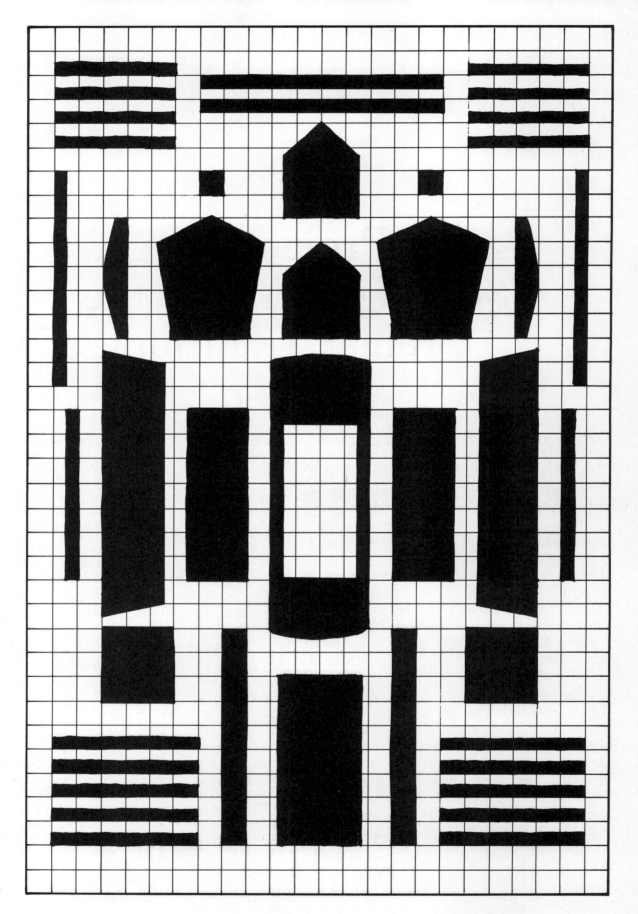

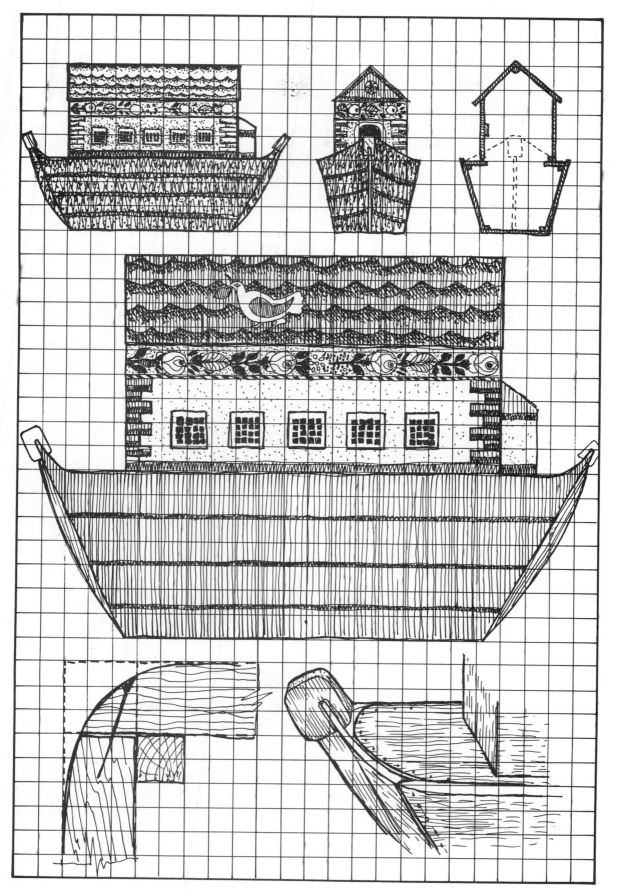

Tools and Materials

For this project you need:

- a quantity of 8"-wide plank wood—it's best to use ³/₄"-thick wood for the hull and ¹/₂"-thick wood for the house and the upper deck;
- a good selection of off cuts, including small-section strips and beadings;
- a quantity of stiff, corrugated grocery-carton cardboard;
- a roll of masking tape—or you can use reinforced carton-sealing tape or clear tape;
- a tenon saw;
- a coping saw;
- a rasp;
- a small hammer;
- a ¹/₄"-wide chisel;
- a cutting board and a metal straightedge;
- a pencil and measure;
- PVA wood glue;
- a quantity of ³/₄"- and 1"-long brads;
- a scalpel;
- a large pair of scissors;
- a quantity of stencil-plate cardboard—you can use varnished cardboard or even clear plastic acetate;
- a small hand drill with a selection of fine bits;
- a good selection of acrylic paints;
- a selection of brushes, including long-haired fine-point brushes and short-haired stencil brushes;
- a pack of graded sandpapers;
- varnish; and
- all the usual workshop items, such as newspaper, old cloths, and throwaway paint containers.

Making the Prototype

Take a good look at Illus. 133, noting the prow-to-stern measurement of 22 inches; then, with the grocery-carton cardboard, masking tape, and scissors, begin to build a prototype. It's best to start by establishing the size of the main areas—the base, the deck, and the hull sides—and then to build the rest of the form to suit. Don't worry too much at this stage about details, such as the slight curving at the corners of the hull, because you can really only take care of them when you are working with a wood thickness; just try to work out the size and shape of

the main templates. By trial and error—that is, by building on, cutting away, and modifying—gradually work towards creating a good stable form. With a prow-to-stern measurement of 22", you need to end up with an Ark that measures about 12" along the base, 6" from the base to the upper deck, 5" from the deck to the eaves, and 8" from the deck to the point of the roof. Of course, there's no reason why these measurements can't be modified slightly, but try to stay within the overall symmetry and proportion of the project.

When you have before you a good cardboard mock-up, or prototype, take note of all the critical measurements, and then very carefully use the scalpel to cut the form down. The actual sides of the prototype can be used as templates. You need to finish up with templates for the base, the four hull sides, the main deck, the sides and ends of the house, the roof, and the little shapes that make up the porch. When this is done, label the templates *end*, *stern*, and so on, making a point of labelling all working faces and mating edges.

Building the Hull

Use ¹/₂"-thick wood for the base and the main deck, and ³/₄"-thick wood for the hull sides. It's best to use soft wood. Working with the saw and rasp, start cutting the base. When the base is set, cut and work the two hull sides.

With the sides in position on the base, lean them out at the top so as to obtain the characteristic hull form; then adjust the side-to-base fit by cutting the bottom side edges at an angle. With the sides of the hull adjusted so that they are canted out at the top edge, attach them by gluing and nailing up through the base.

Having first set the shape of the hull by nailing a couple of temporary holding strips across the sides (Illus. 134), take the two end boards (the prow and stern boards), and modify them to fit. As with the hull sides, the end boards need to be angled at the bottom edge so that they sit well on the base; but, also, they need to be cut so that they fit nicely between the canted sides. Rasp and sand the edges of the end boards until they are a good, tight fit between the base and the sides, and then glue and nail them. Noting that the vertical corners of the

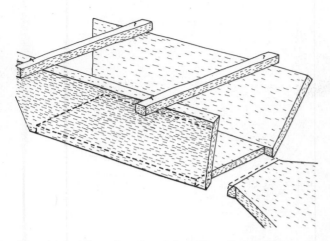

Illus. 134. Adjust the sides of the hull so that they are canted outward, and nail temporary holding strips across the sides.

hull need to be rounded, make sure that you countersink the nails and place them well back from the edges of the wood. Strengthen the inside angles with off-cut strips bedded in glue, wait overnight for the glue to dry, and then use the rasp to round off the corners. If you have used 3/4"-thick wood for the sides of the hull, you will be able cut back and round the wood at the corners so that the prow and the stern boards appear to be bowed. When this is done, take the rasp and reduce the thickness of the wood along the top edge of both the prow and the stern. Shape and curve the top edge of the boards so that they run in a smooth curve through to the side boards.

Now, bearing in mind that the main deck is cut from 1/2"-thick wood and needs to be placed so that it is set just a fraction of an inch lower than the top edge of the sides of the Ark, nail and glue a beading around the inside of the hull. When the glue is dry, cut and modify the main deck so that it comes to rest on the beading, fitting good and snug like a lid (Illus. 135). Then cut the main-deck hatchway. Finally, take a piece of sandpaper and rub the hull down to a smooth splinter-free finish.

Building the House

When the hull is finished, use the template, the saws, and the 1/2"-thick wood, and cut out all the shapes that make up the house—the two gable walls, the two long walls, the two roof panels, and the little porch pieces.

When you have checked all the sizes off against your working drawings and templates, take the two gable walls, the two roof pieces, and the long wall (meaning the long fixed wall), and build the basic house form. Nail and glue the long side wall onto the gable walls, cap the gables with the roof, and strengthen all the inside angles with beading off cuts bedded in glue. When the glue is dry, take the other long wall (meaning the sliding-door wall), and chamfer it along the top edge so that it is cut back at the same angle as the roof. Now, nail a door-guide strip along the underside of the roof. Noting the distance between the roof eaves and the surface of the deck, and realizing the need for the door to run in a grooved deck track, chamfer the door along its bottom edge. Use the straight saw and the 1/4"-wide chisel to cut the deck track.

Now, having first made sure that the sliding door has a good, smooth-running fit and that the house is square, support the house upside down on the work surface, dribble glue on the bottom edge of the three fixed walls, place the main-deck board on the up-turned house, check to be sure that the hatchway is aligned, and then attach the deck to the house with brads. Strengthen the inside deck-to-wall angles with glued and nailed off cuts, and attach the little porch on the end of the house. When this is done, set the deck on the hull, and attach it in place with glue and nails. Finally, attach the prow, the stern,

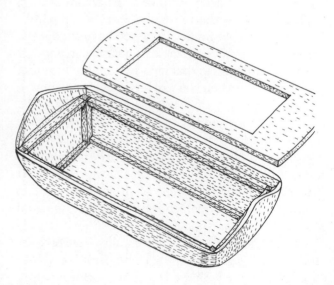

Illus. 135. Use a rasp to round off the corners, and cut the main deck to fit.

129

and the keel strips and blocks (Illus. 136), and rub the whole Ark down to a smooth finish.

Working the Stencils

Look at Illus. 133 and 137, and see how you need five main stencil plates—one for the roof pattern, one for the dove, one for the floral pattern, and two for the windows.

Start by applying a primer, an undercoat, and the main areas of ground color. Consider painting the roof a light brown, the patterned strip under the eaves a rich emerald green, the walls of the house a gray, the deck a light green and the hull a dark brown. While the paint is drying, select one of the stencilled areas and draw the design.

For instance, if you are working on the windows, first note the way the window pattern is made up from a grid of 16 little squares, and then use work-out paper, a pencil, and a ruler to draw the design accordingly. When you have achieved a good design, trace it off, and then, with a pencil, press-transfer the traced lines through to the working face of the stencil cardboard. Identify the areas that need to be cut away; in this case, it's the squares. Then use a metal straightedge and a scalpel to clear away the waste. Working on a cutting board, and making sure that your fingertips are well clear of the scalpel, clear way the small squares of cardboard with a series of clean, straight cuts. Now, take another look at Illus. 137 and see how the 16 small squares are set within a larger square, or frame. Once you have cut out the 16 squares in the stencil cardboard, cut another piece of cardboard so that it corresponds to the outer window frame; then you will have two stencil plates, one for the outer frame and one for the little squares. When you have cut the two stencil plates, establish where on the sides of the house you are going to place the windows, and draw in a few registration marks. Now, take the stencil plate for the outer frame, place it on the side of the house, and dab white paint in the frame. Repeat this process with all 10 windows. You should have 10 blind white windows set against the gray of the walls—five on each side of the house. When the white paint is dry, take the stencil plate with the 16 squares, locate it within one of the blind white windows, hold it in place with tabs of masking tape, and then use the small stencil

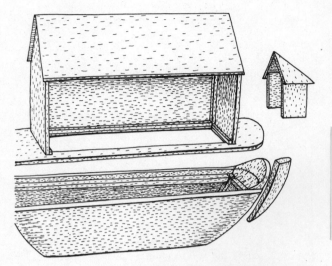

Illus. 136. Nail and glue the house and porch onto the main deck; then attach the deck on the hull, and apply the keel strips and blocks.

brush and the black paint to dab in the design (Illus. 138). It's all fairly easy and straightforward, as long as you make sure to use a nearly dry brush, to place the area being stencilled so that it's flat and horizontal, and to make positive stabs with the brush.

Continue in this manner with the other stencils—the wavy-line stencil that makes up the roof design, the floral stencil, and the dove. Of course, each design will have its own problems, but the basic stencil process is always the same: You draw the design, press-transfer the traced design with a pencil through to the stencil cardboard, cut out the "windows" of the design, secure the stencil cardboard on the area to be decorated, paint in the cut "windows" with a dryish brush, and then carefully peel up the stencil plate.

Painting and Finishing

When you have blocked in all the stencilled areas—meaning the windows, the wavy-roof pattern, the dove, and the large yellow and white flowers and green foliage areas within the floral pattern—then clear away the stencil plates and all the other work-

On the opposite page: Illus. 137. Working-drawing stencil-plate grid. The scale is about four grid squares to 1". Top: roof stencil. Second from top: dove stencils. Second from bottom: flowers stencil. Bottom: windows stencils.

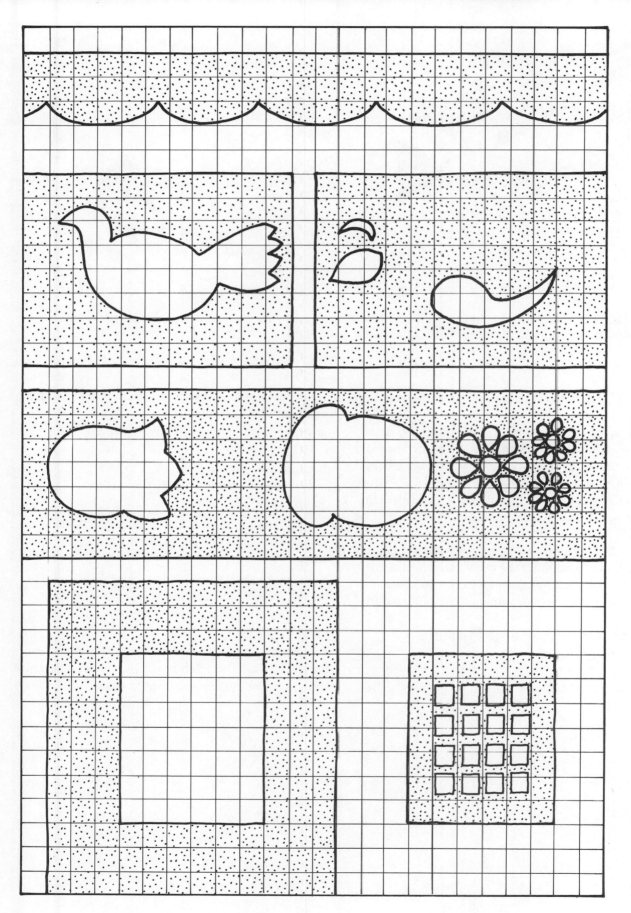

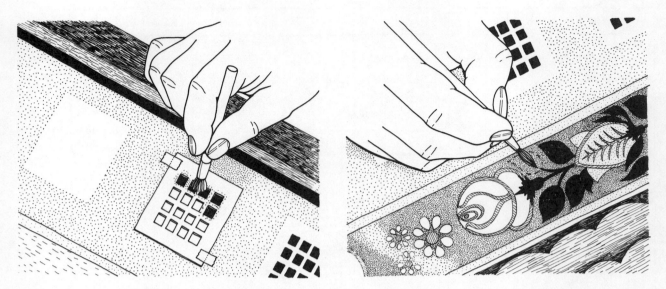

Illus. 138 (left). Secure the inner-window stencil plate with tabs of masking tape, and then dab in the holes with a stencil brush and slightly dry paint. Illus. 139 (right). Bring out the details of the stencilled frieze with a fine-point brush and a little bit of paint.

surface clutter, and set out your paints and the fine-point brushes.

Now, go over the Ark, highlighting the details and embellishing the hard-edged stencil-worked forms. Fill in the dove's wing with blue, use emerald green for the leaf in its beak, put little dabs of white and red in and around the flowers (Illus. 139), define the stone cornices with fine lines, put a black line around the white window frame, add a stripe for the plinth line around the base of the house, paint a little dashed line under the floral pattern, and so on. Finally, put your name and date on the base, and give the entire piece a couple of coats of varnish.

Troubleshooting and Possible Modifications

• If you decide to use thinner wood for the hull, then you will have to settle for squarer corners and a flat prow and stern boards because you won't be able to cut away the wood thickness.

• Be warned, if you scrub the brush backwards and forward, the paint will run under the stencil plate, and if you use runny paint, the designs will run beyond their boundaries.

• Use a sharp scalpel to cut the stencil plates. The edges of the plates need to be smooth, clean-cut, and crisp.

• It's best to use acrylic paints because they dry so quickly. However, you can also use fast-drying spray paints. If you don't mind slow-drying paints, try using model makers' enamels.

• Because acrylics do dry out so fast, it's important for you to wash the brushes and the stencil plates as soon as possible after you've used them.

Project 2
Making a Lathe-Turned Figure in the Cremer Tradition

Design, Structure, and Technique Considerations

Look at Mrs. Noah, with her stern straight back, high bosom, slender waist, leg-o'-mutton sleeves, and high-crowned brimmed hat—and Mr. Noah, with his open, honest face and rounded hat (Illus. 140). With their untroubled naïve expressions, these Cremer Ark figures have been described as being the archetype of the Western wood-carved doll.

Take a look at the accompanying drawings and the drawing on page D in the color section, and see how the wonderfully fluid and yet restrained forms are first turned on the lathe and then carved and painted. Note how the skittle figures stand directly on their turned bases, and how both Mr. and Mrs. Noah have cutaway backs. See, also, how the figures are turned off all in one piece and then built up by having movable split-bobbin arms attached on a pivotal dowel rod through their bodies—meaning that the arms are glued on the ends of the dowel so that they can be swung up and down.

Spend some time searching out wood-carved dolls and Ark figures in toy museums; then make sketches, showing the various forms, colors, and sizes. When this is done, study the accompanying illustrations, noting the two basic male and female designs. Then, with a pencil and work-out paper, either copy our traditional designs directly or play

Illus. 140. Project picture. Mr. and Mrs. Noah are about 4" high. Note the pivotal arms, the cut-away detailing of the chest, and the hat and dress forms.

around with the details and see if you can come up with some exciting modifications. In Illus. 141 and 142, note how at four grid squares to 1", our figures work out to be about 1½" in diameter at the base and 4" in height; then draw your templates accordingly. Although this project only describes in detail how to make a male figure—meaning Mr. Noah or one of his three sons—when you come to making the womenfolk, all you need to do is change the turning and carving details.

Tools and Materials

For this project you need:

- an easy-to-turn piece of wood that is about 1½" X 1½" square and 5" to 6" long for the body—consider using lime, holly, or a piece of straight-grained pine;
- a small scrap of wood for the arms;
- the use of a small lathe, with either a three-jaw chuck or perhaps a dowel-holding special chuck;
- a selection of turning tools;
- the use of a workbench and vise;
- a small straight saw;
- a pair of callipers;
- a small hand drill with two drill bits, one at $^3/_{16}$" and the other at ¼";
- a measure;
- a pack of graded sandpapers;
- a sharp whittling knife or scalpel;
- a wood primer;
- a good selection of acrylic paints;
- brushes;
- glue;
- varnish;
- cardboard;
- scissors; and
- a pad of work-out paper.

Making the Templates and Roughing Out

Having noted all the designing and building details, sit down with your pad of work-out paper and finalize your designs. Establish the overall height and width, the size of the head and hat, and the position of the arms, and then carefully draw a full-size working plan, or illustration. Take a tracing, and, with a pencil, press-transfer the traced lines through to a piece of cardboard; then cut out a template.

Now, pin up your design and illustrations, set out your tools, and generally make sure that your work area is safe and organized. When this is done, find the end-of-wood center points by marking off corner-to-corner diagonals, and secure the wood on the lathe by mounting it between the fork center, or prong chuck, and the dead center of the tailstock. Spin the wood, just to make sure that it's running true. Then bring the tool rest up to the wood and secure it so that the top of the rest is a little above the height of the lathe center. Now, using the tools of your choice, switch on the lathe and work backwards and forward along the length of the spinning wood, clearing away the waste. Try to turn the wood down to a smooth 1¼" diameter (Illus. 143).

Cutting the Profiles

Take a look at Illus. 141 and see how, from bottom to top, the Mr. Noah shape sits on a broad base, tapers upwards to 1"-diameter shoulders, is reduced down to a slender neck, is opened up for the hat brim, and, finally, is rounded over the hat crown.

Having noted how halfway along the cone-shaped body the otherwise-smooth profile is interrupted by a belt ring, or bead, take your callipers and side skew chisel, and clear away the rough. Working with the grain—that is, from large to small diameter—try to achieve a 4"-long truncated cone—a cone that springs out of a 1¼"-diameter base and tapers to a flat 1"-diameter apex. Using the callipers to mark off the position of the belt ring and noting how there is a $^1/_{16}$" step up from the main body of the cone to the ring, make incisions and reduce the diameter of the cone accordingly.

Now, still using the template, callipers, and the

On the following pages: Illus. 141. Working-drawing grid for Mr. Noah. The scale is about four grid squares to 1". Note the attachment of the arms through the body, the all-of-a-piece turning, and the way the arms are worked from a split turning. Illus. 142. Working-drawing grid for Mrs. Noah. The scale is about four grid squares to 1". The details are the same as for Mr. Noah.

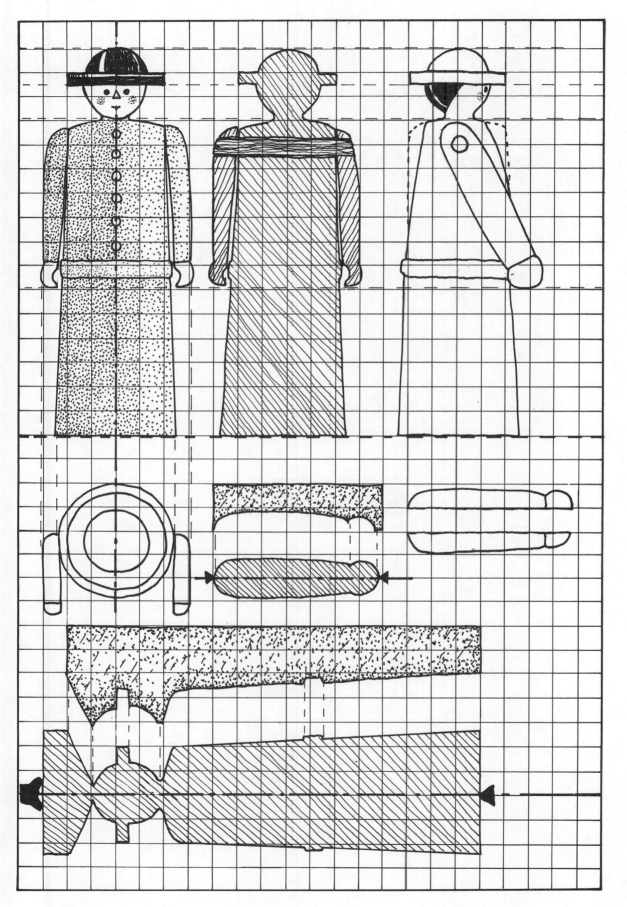

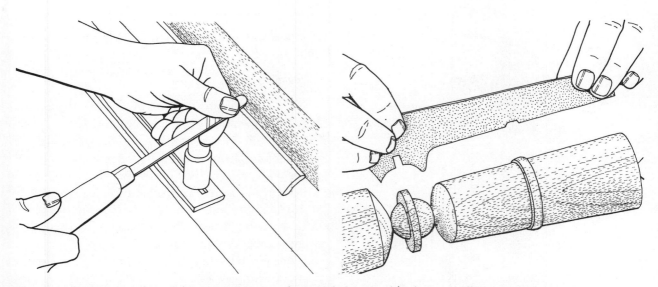

Illus. 143 (left). Secure the wood between centers and turn it down to a 1¼" diameter. Illus. 144 (right). Using the template as a guide, turn off the various dips, beads, and curves that make up the form.

tools of your choice, turn off the waste at the neck, shoulders, and hat crown (Illus. 144). But remember, before you reach the hat crown, to leave the ⅛"-thick, 1"-diameter hat brim standing out in high relief. Finally, take the wood to a good smooth finish and part off.

Making the Arms

Set the wood in the jaws of your chosen chuck, making sure that all is secure and running true, and

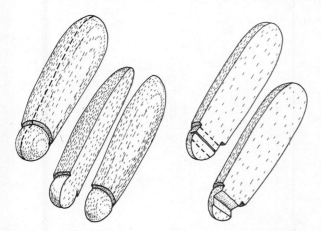

Illus. 145. To make the arms (from left to right), turn off the little arm shape, split the turning down its length, and cut in the V-section palms.

then swiftly turn down the rough until you have achieved the simple 1¾"-long, ½"-diameter, round-ended arm profile. Next, take the wood to a smooth finish, cut in the cuff and the ball-shaped fist, and part off.

When this is done, take the straight saw, set the little sausage shape on top of the slightly open jaws of the vise, and then very carefully halve, or split, the turned section along its length. Now, a piece at a time, take the split turnings, hold them sawn-face down on a sheet of sandpaper, and work them to a good finish.

Finally, take a knife and with three cuts—meaning a single central stop cut and two slanting cuts—chop out a V-shaped notch on the inside hand, or palm, area (Illus. 145).

Carving, Cutting, and Putting the Parts Together

Clear away all the waste and bench clutter, and set out the pieces that make up the figure—the body, the two arms, and the 1¾"-long piece of 3/16"-diameter dowel. Take a good look at Illus. 141 (or Illus. 142) and note carefully how the arms are placed in relationship to the body. Then place the arms side by side and with the flat face down on the work surface, and mark the position of the pivotal hole at the top of each arm. Leaving about ¼" of wood

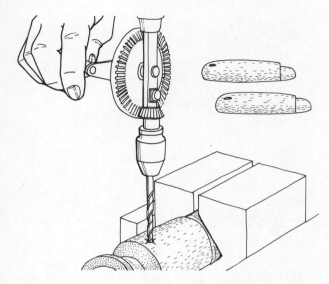

Illus. 146. When you drill the holes, use a 3/16" bit for the arms and a 1/4" bit for the body.

this is done, take the main skittle-turned body, establish where the arms are to be pivoted, and then, with the pencil and the 1/4" bit, mark and drill the wood accordingly.

Now, use a sharp knife to slice away the waste from the chest and the back of the figure (Illus. 147). Cutting from the waist to the shoulders, try to leave the chest and the back of the figure, more or less, flat. Work with caution, being extra careful so that the knife won't slip out of control and damage the wood at the head and hat brim. It's best to hold the figure so that the head is nearest you and to work with a thumb-controlled paring cut.

Once you have taken the top half of the figure to a smooth knife-worked finish, slide the dowel rod through the body, decide which side of the body is front or back, and then push the arms on the ends of the dowel. If all is well, and the dowel is a loose fit in the body and a tight fit in the arm holes, glue the arms in position and whittle back the ends of the dowel (Illus. 147).

between the top of the arm and the side of the hole, drill the arm holes with the 3/16"-diameter bit. When

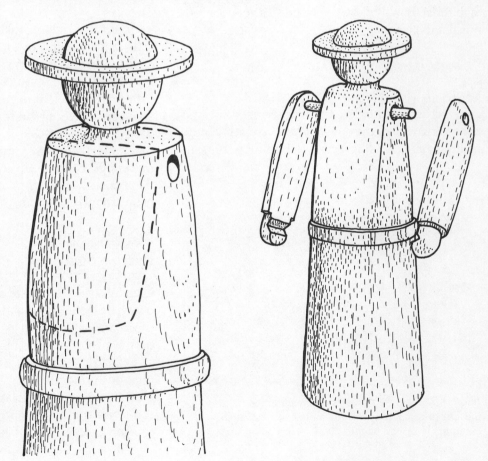

Illus. 147. Left: Use a sharp knife to slice away the chest waste. Right: Slide the dowel rod through the body and glue the arms in place.

138

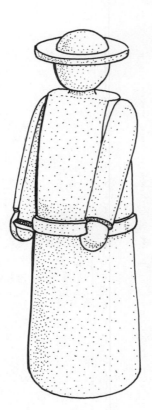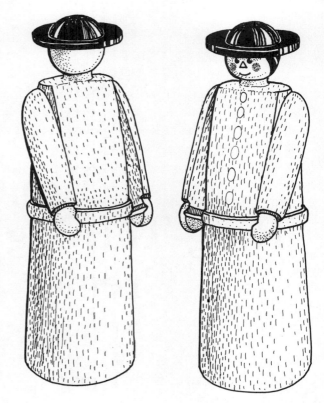

Illus. 148. Left: Apply a primer and undercoat. Middle: Paint the shoulders-to-base blue, and the hat black. Right: Paint the buttons white, the cheeks and mouth red, and the eyes and nose black.

Painting and Finishing

When the glue is dry, apply a primer and an undercoat over the entire workpiece. Then add a blue top coat from the base to the shoulders, and a black top coat on the hat.

Wait a short while for the acrylic paint to harden, and then use a fine-point brush and small amounts of white, red, black, and yellow paint to dab in the details of the buttons, cheeks, eyes, nose, mouth, and belt (Illus. 148). Don't try for subtle realistic features; it's much better to dash them in as swiftly and directly as possible, and then to move on to the next figure to be painted.

When the paint is dry, make sure that the arms swing freely and, if necessary, use a scalpel to cut back hard blobs of dry paint. Then give the whole figure a couple of coats of gloss varnish.

Troubleshooting and Possible Modifications

• Although the turning is fairly straightforward, you need to work the hat brim with extra care and make sure that your turning tools are sharp.

• When you are carving the back and chest, be careful so that the knife doesn't slip out of control and run into the hat brim.

• Although the arms are hanging straight down and are loosely pivotted, there's no reason why you couldn't modify the project and have the arms either glued to the body or loosely pivoted so that, say, one arm is up and the other is down.

• You might consider dipping the body and the arms in paint before you put the figure together.

Project 3
Ring-Turning a Zebra in the Cremer Tradition

Design, Structure, and Technique Considerations

Also known as *Equus burchelli*, the zebra is a beautiful animal that belongs to the horse family. Standing about 4 feet high at the shoulders, with long ears, a tail, a thin covering of hair, and, of course, the wonderful counterchange striping, the zebra is not, as most people suppose, a black-and-white striped animal, or even a black animal with white stripes, but rather it's white with black stripes.

If you look at all the illustrations pertaining to the animals in this section, you'll see that they are all made on the lathe using the German ring method. With this method, a small-tree section is first selected and prepared for turning, and then, on the lathe, the blank is turned down to a true disc. Next, using various gouges and templates, the disc is shaped, reversed, and reworked until it appears to be correctly profiled. This technique may seem difficult, but, in fact, it's relatively easy and straightforward. However, prior to turning, the animal shapes do need to be simplified, and, also, since the shape of the animal can't be seen during turning, it's necessary to make templates.

When the basic ring, or tube, section has been turned off, it is taken from the lathe and then sawn or chopped radially. It is these slices, or segments, that are shaped like an animal. Look at Illus. 151 and see how, if the animals are to come out correctly wedge-shaped—that is, narrow at the head and wide at the rear—the ring needs to be worked so that the zebra looks towards the center. Since you probably don't want an entire ringful of, say, 30 zebras, don't

Illus. 149. Project picture. The zebra is about 3" long and 2½" high. Note that it needs to be attached to a base.

Illus. 150. Inspirational drawing. You might want to modify the zebra form and make other horse- and deer-like animals. Top left: European red deer. Top right: Shetland pony. Middle left: Asian wild ass. Middle right: North African addax. Bottom left: Sardinian dwarf donkey. Bottom right: North American elk or moose.

worry because you can modify the individual ring slices by whittling them smaller or by adding bits and pieces, such as horns or antlers, to make them into, say, horses, ponies, mules, donkeys, deer, large dogs, or whatever. With some imaginative forethought, you will be able make a dozen, or so, different animals from one basic section. Certainly, you do need the use of a small lathe, but rest assured because the process is neither lengthy nor difficult.

Tools and Materials

For this project you need:
- a piece of half-seasoned small-tree section wood

that is about 5" to 6" thick and 12" in diameter, meaning a prepared 5" to 6" slice, or blank, taken from a 12"-diameter log, or tree—you can use lime, beech, a fruit wood, or any other easy-to-turn wood;
- the use of a small lathe;
- a faceplate;
- a screwdriver and screws to fit the faceplate;
- a 5"-thick, 15"-diameter disc of rough wood for a wooden chuck;
- a selection of turning tools;
- a small coping saw;
- a long knife—you can use an old carving knife, an axe, or even an old plane iron;
- a mallet;
- a firm, level tree-stump chopping block;
- a couple of whittling knives;
- a hand drill with a $\frac{1}{8}$"-diameter drill bit;
- an inch, or so, of cord;
- PVA glue;
- work-out and tracing paper;
- a quantity of stiff cardboard;
- scissors;
- a measure and callipers;
- primer and undercoat;
- acrylic paint;
- varnish;
- a selection of brushes; and
- items, such as cloths, paint containers, and sandpaper.

Making the Templates

First, study traditional Ark zebras, modern plastic-toy zebras, and zebras in zoos, and clip various photographs of zebras from magazines. Then look at Illus. 151 and see how you need to make three profile templates. Note how, at a scale of four grid squares to 1", our zebra is about 3" long and 2 $\frac{1}{2}$" high; then take your work-out paper and draw what you consider to be a good template profile. First, draw a detailed zebra—complete with ears, hooves, and fetlocks—and then modify the shape so as to sim-

On the following page: Illus. 151. Working drawing. Top: The scale is about four grid squares to 1". Note the zebra in relation to the turned ring.

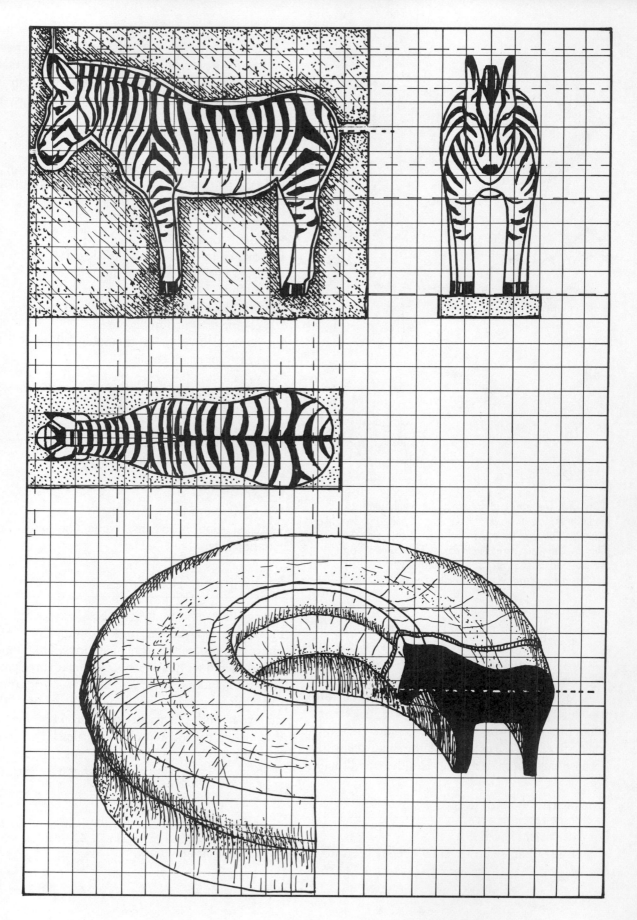

plify the outline. Noting how the templates need to be worked so that they can be easily pushed up against the wood being turned and then just as easily withdrawn, establish a strong, uncomplicated outline.

Once you have achieved a design that encompasses all the project requirements, make a tracing and, with a pencil, press-transfer the traced lines through to a piece of fairly stiff cardboard. Arrange the zebra outline so that it is set square with the sides of the cardboard; draw in the template breaks at the ears, tail, and hooves; and then take the scissors and make the three cutouts. Label the working faces and edge breaks of the three pieces of cardboard so that you will be able to easily identify and reassemble them.

Turning Off the First Half

Make sure that the lathe is in good working order; then roll up your sleeves, pin up your designs, and set out your tools so that they are close at hand.

Now, take the prepared blank and screw it to the faceplate, being sure to locate the screws in areas of waste. When you have checked to see that the wood is secure, mount the faceplate on the lathe and use the tools of your choice to bring the blank to a swift trim. When the wood is running true, take the template for the legs, the callipers, and a round-nose turning tool, and make sweeps from the center to the side to clear away the waste (Illus. 152). Turn out the wood from the line of the front hooves around to the nose, from between the legs, and from the line of the back hooves around to the tail. As you are working, stop every once in a while and test the profiles with the template and the callipers.

When the face of the turning fits the template, take the graded sandpapers and rub the wood down to a smooth finish. Finally, pencil the position of the template break points on the turning—that is, the break points on the nostrils and the tail.

Chuck-Turning

When you have turned off one face of the blank— meaning the whole underside profile of the zebra from the tail, around the legs, up the chest, and through to the nostrils—take the wood off the faceplate.

Now, mount the large piece of chuck wood on the faceplate and swiftly cut it back to a smooth, true trim. Take a calliper reading of the back-legs diameter from the half-worked zebra, and then hollow-turn the chuck to fit. Turn out a smooth-sided, slightly tapered recess, into which the zebra ring legs can be set. When you have achieved a tight push fit, make sure that the zebra ring is secure and running true, and then proceed to turn off the top half of the zebra's profile. Start by piercing the wood at its center and turning out the waste from around the

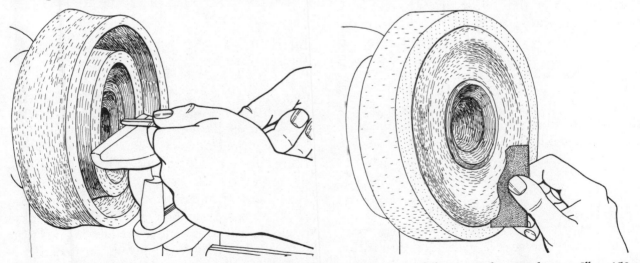

Illus. 152 (left). With the blank well secured on the faceplate, turn off the legs and clear away the central waste. Illus. 153 (right). Wedge the legs side of the ring in the wooden chuck and turn off the waste. Use the back template to make sure that the turning is to size.

143

zebra's nose; while you do this, be careful not to dig the tool into the wood and jar it off true. When you have turned out the nostrils and ears to a good template fit, check again, just to make sure that the wood is still secure and running true, and then turn off the waste from the tips of the ears to the tail (Illus. 153).

When you have cleared the wood from the nostrils, right up and over the head, and then down and around the tail, carefully ease the ring out of the chuck and check its profile with the templates. If all is well, the three templates should just about touch at the break points. Of course, if you have cut away too much wood, then there's not much you can do except perhaps modify the form or chalk it all up to experience. However, if the profile is too large or proud, then all you need to do is cross-hatch the areas that need to be cut back, remount the wood on the lathe, and carefully skim off the waste until all three templates come together in a good fit. Finally, use the graded sandpapers to rub the wood down to a good, smooth finish.

Cutting the Ring

When the ring is well-turned, carefully ease it out of the chuck, place it the right way up on the chopping block, and set out your knife (or axe) and the mallet. Carefully position the knife so that it lines up with the center of the ring, and then give the back of the blade a tap with the mallet. Make two cuts to split the ring in half. Take one half-ring, use the compass to make 1"-wide step-offs around the outer circumference, and then begin to work with the knife and the mallet, striking off 1"-wide radial wedge slices (Illus. 154). Note: If you start with a 12"-diameter blank, you should end up with about 36 profile slices, with each zebra slice being approximately 1" wide at the rear and ½" wide at the nose.

Whittling

Clear your work surface of all clutter, reject any zebra slices that appear to be damaged (that is, any that are split or knotty), and set out your knives. Now, bearing in mind that you will be making some of the

slices into other animals, such as horses or donkeys, select two nicely profiled slices and stand them upright on the work surface so that you can see them in plan, or top, view.

With one eye on your working drawings, take a soft pencil and carefully sketch the zebra outline on the top of the two slices. Draw the curve of the rump, the belly, and the narrowing of the neck. When this is done, look at the zebra from both the front and back, and mark in the areas of waste between the legs.

Make several checks, just to make sure that all is correct; then, a slice at a time, set the zebras upside down in the jaws of a muffled vise and use the coping saw to clear away the waste. Being careful not to twist or force the blade and thus split the wood, first

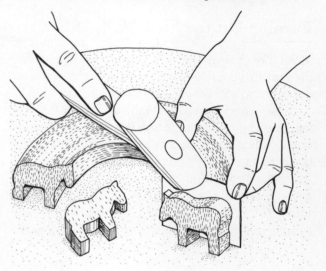

Illus. 154. Use a mallet and either a knife or an old plane iron to cut off the radial wedge slices.

make a pilot cut straight down between the legs, and then make two inside-leg cuts down into the pilot cut. When you have roughed out the legs, take one of the whittling knives and start to carve away the smaller areas of waste. Shape up both sides of the slice until the zebra begins to look nicely rounded (Illus. 155). Then cut out the notch of waste between the ears, detail the eyes, round off the flanks, slice in the tail crease, and so on. Bear in mind that since the grain runs vertically from the hoof to the back, there will be fragile areas of short grain around the nostrils and the ears. Gradually work towards creating a good form. Then, with a scalpel and sandpaper, take the zebra to a smooth, detailed finish.

Painting and Finishing

Clear away all the waste, make sure that your entire work area is free from dust, and set out your paints and brushes. Now, remembering to give the paint time to dry out between coats, apply a primer, an undercoat, and a base of gloss white. Before you go any further, take a good long look at Illus. 149 and at your various drawings and photographs, and see how the zebra is indeed a white animal with black stripes. Note the black mane and nose, the way the black lines run from the top of the back and down

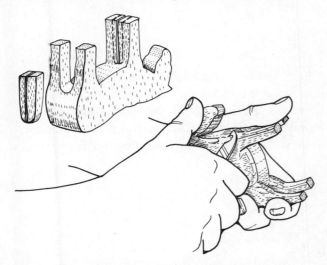

Illus. 155. Top: Clear away the between-the-leg waste. Bottom: Use a knife to model and round off the sharp angles.

under the belly, the way the body markings change direction when they meet at the top of the legs, and the way the stripes become pointed as they near the tail.

Once you've become familiar with the markings, mix a small amount of blue-black paint by adding just enough blue to the black to give it a slight blue tinge. When you come to painting the blue-black stripes on the main body, it's best to set the paint-loaded brush down at the mane, to run the stripes down the flanks, and to lift the brush off at the belly so that the stripes come to a fine-pointed finish.

Finally, when the paint is dry, drill a 1/8"-diameter tail hole, glue and peg-attach the cord tail, and give the finished zebra a generous coat of varnish.

Troubleshooting and Possible Modifications

• A chuck refers to just about any type of wood-holding device used on the lathe. Although we have decided to make and use a wooden chuck, you can use a three-jawed metal chuck or even a chuck special. Check with your lathe supplier.

• If you plan on turning off a lot of rings, it's best to make the chuck from a good strong wood, such as beech.

• You can also make the templates from either metal-sheet or thin plywood.

• For safety's sake, before you switch on the lathe, make sure that your cuffs, tie, hair, and such are well out of the way.

• When you want to test a profile with one of the templates, switch off the lathe and wait until the spinning wood comes to rest.

• If you don't like the idea of splitting the turned ring with an axe or knife, then try using a saw.

Project 4
Ring-Turning a Lion in the Cremer Tradition

Design, Structure, and Technique Considerations

The Bible is full of references to lions; for instance, Samson took some honey from a lion, David killed a lion, Daniel was cast into a den full of lions, a couple of the prophets were eaten by lions, and Satan was likened to a lion. Nowadays lions are only found in the wilds of Africa and India, but a hundred, or so, years ago, they also lived in parts of Europe and

Illus. 156. Project picture. The lion is about 3½" long and 2" high.

Illus. 157. Inspirational drawing. If you like the idea of making big cats, there are quite a few to choose from. Top: African lion, a female. Second from top, left: African genet. Second from top, right: Indian tiger. Middle: South American jaguar. Bottom: African cheetah.

Syria. So, the original Ark makers knew all about the King of the Beasts.

As to how the male lion came to symbolize pride, courage, and strength, it's quite a mystery, especially since he is characteristically a peaceful beast who likes nothing better than to eat a large meal that his mate has caught and then have a long lazy sleep. Nevertheless, lions have always been associated with danger. Thus, since the Ark makers knew that children enjoy playing with scary animals, they always included quite a few of the big cats in their Arks.

Imagine a shadowy lamp-lit Victorian playroom—the children are playing with their Ark. Can't you just see the hundred, or so, animals all lined up on the carpet: lions that live in deepest darkest Africa, wonderfully striped man-eating tigers, leopards with their never-changing spots, panthers with their hot-coal eyes, jaguars, cougars, and cheetahs that can run 70 miles per hour. What fun! What excitement!

Now, take a look at the accompanying illustrations and consider how the mass-production ring-turning method of making many animals of one type is also ideally suited for making lots of similar beasts. So, even though this project only specifically describes how to turn off a male-lion ring, once this ring is made you will be able to take the individual "cat" slices and modify them with a knife and a paint brush to make tigers, leopards, and all the rest.

Note how, for the lion, you need to make four templates—one that runs from the nose to the tail, one that follows around from the nose to the bottom of the front foot, one that goes from the front foot around the belly and down to the back foot, and, lastly, one that maps out the shape from the back foot to the tail. See how, with the between-the-legs template, you need to simplify the shape of the back leg so that the template can be withdrawn.

When you have a good understanding of all the tool, technique, and material requirements of the project, look over the accompanying illustrations, search out drawings and photos of Ark cats, and then take your pencil and sketchbook and spend some time at the zoo.

Tools and Materials

For this project you need:
- a section of small-tree wood that is about 4" thick and 12" in diameter—consider using a knot-free wood, such as lime, beech, cherry, holly, or soft maple;
- a 4"-thick, 15"-diameter rough-wood blank for the chuck;
- a piece of ¼"-thick wood that is about 2" wide and 3 ½" long for the base;
- a good selection of turning tools;
- a small coping saw;
- a straight saw;
- a couple of whittling knives, including a sharp, pointed penknife and a fine-point scalpel;
- a hand drill and a ⅛"-diameter drill bit;

147

- an inch, or so, of brown cord;
- a small quantity of PVA wood glue;
- work-out and tracing paper;
- a measure and callipers;
- a pair of dividers;
- a quantity of stiff cardboard;
- a pair of scissors;
- primer and an undercoat;
- acrylic paints, in yellow, brown, and green;
- varnish;
- a selection of brushes; and
- all the usual workshop items, such as cloths, newspaper, and sandpaper.

Designing the Templates

Take a look at Illus. 156 and see how the lion has a tight profile, meaning that the legs and neck are short and the overall shape is compact. Note that at a grid scale of four squares to 1" (Illus. 158), the lion is about 3 ½" from nose to tail and about 2" high.

Now, take your pencil and work-out paper, and draw your own design. First, establish the lion's profile—complete with mane, ear, and joint details—and then simplify the form until you have reduced the shape down to its essentials. Aim for a smooth, well-proportioned workable generalization. When you have achieved a good, bold profile of a male lion, take a tracing and, with a pencil, press-transfer the traced lines through to the working face of the piece of template cardboard. For ease of working, it's best to position the lion so that he is set square with the cardboard. When this is done, draw in the break lines at the feet, nose, and tail, and then cut out the four templates. Label or color-code the templates to avoid confusion.

Turning the Legs

When you have made your templates, inspect your wood, just to make sure that it is completely free from troublesome flaws, such as knots, splits, and sappy edges. Then mount the 12"-diameter blank on a faceplate, and the faceplate on the lathe. First, check to make sure that both the stop and start switches work, the tailstock is out of the way, the tool rest is a firm fixture and not touching the work,

the tools are close at hand, and your hair and clothes are out of harm's way. Then switch on the lathe.

Start by turning off the rough from both the side and the face. Run the round-nosed chisel back and forth along the side, and from side to center across the face, until the blank appears to be running smooth and true. Now, using the templates and the tools of your choice, hollow-turn the side and face waste so as to achieve the deep central hollow and the various grooves and trenches that make up the underside of the lion's profile. Cut back the waste until the templates fit the wood. Then, having had another good look at your drawings and photographs of lions, use a small tool to cut in the finer details of the belly, joint, and foot (Illus. 159).

Chuck Work

When you have shaped up the underside of the lion's profile, take the workpiece off the lathe and remove it from the faceplate. As likely as not, especially if the metal has warmed up and expanded, it will be difficult to unscrew the faceplate from the mandrel; so you might need to wait awhile for the metal to cool down.

Then mount the chuck wood on the faceplate and swiftly turn off the rough until it is running true. Take a calliper reading from the leg diameter of the half-finished lion, and then hollow-turn the wooden chuck to fit. Turn out a slightly tapered hollow that is shaped like a flower pot and is about 1½" deep. When you have made a chuck to take the finished part of the lion's leg profile, make sure the wood is a secure safe fit, and then cut back the top waste (Illus. 160). Start by piercing the wood at its center; then enlarge and cut back the hole until you can see the template break point on the lion's nose. When you have located both the nose and the tail template registration points, gradually turn off the waste from the nose to the back and from the tail to the back until the profile is a good fit.

This part of the project can be a bit tricky, so work with care and caution. Since you are working with

On the opposite page: Illus. 158. Working drawing. Top: The scale is four grid squares to 1".

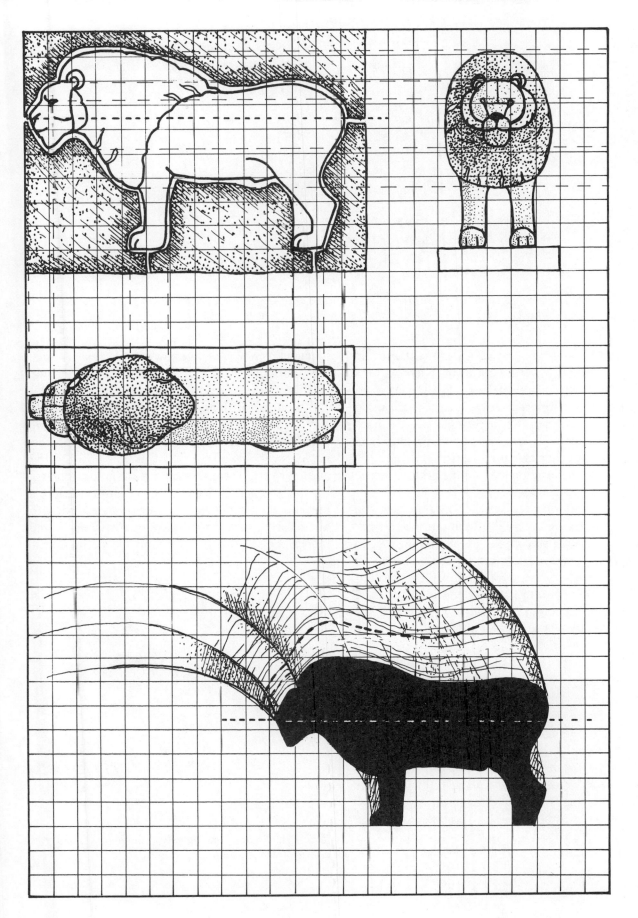

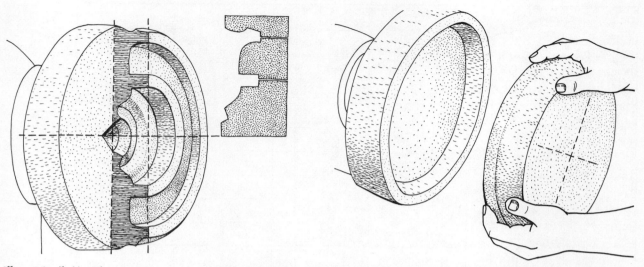

Illus. 159 (left). This cross section shows the half-turned disc and the three-legs template. Illus. 160 (right). Screw the wooden chuck on the faceplate, and check to be sure that the legs side of the ring is a secure fit.

the one template, it's quite difficult to visualize just how much wood has been cut away; therefore, it's best to waste the wood little by little—that is, to make a careful template check, cut back a little more wood, make another check, cut back a little more wood, and so on. When you reach this stage, the more template checks you make the better.

When you have achieved a good profile, ease the ring out of the chuck and check it for a complete template fit. Stand the ring on edge, and test the sections by trying to fit the four templates right around the lion. Using small tabs of masking tape to bridge the template breaks, try to encircle the section with a complete template ring, or bracelet. Finally, when you have turned the wood off to a good fit, use the graded sandpapers to rub the spinning wood down to a smooth finish.

Cutting and Carving

Ease the ring out of the chuck, set it down on your work surface, and then prepare to work with a straightedge, pencil, compass or dividers, and saw. Having first carefully drawn a side-to-side diameter line that passes through the center of the ring, set the dividers to about 1¼" and work around the outer edge of the ring, stepping off the individual slices. Allowing for wastage, count on stepping off about 30 slices. The individual wedge shapes should be about 1¼" wide at the tail end and about ¾" wide at

the head. When you have marked off the slices, take the small straight saw and work around the ring, cutting off the little lion-shaped profiles (Illus. 161).

When this is done, select two of the best slices and set the other 28, or so, aside. At a later date, these will be made into more lions, tigers, leopards, or whatever. Take a good look at Illus. 156 and 157 and your various drawings and photographs, and see how, in shape and size, a lioness is different from a male lion. Then take one of the lion slices and, with a few paring cuts, chop away the heavy mane and reduce the wood slightly around the girth and the

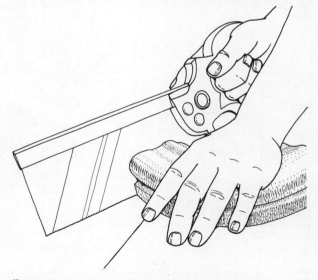

Illus. 161. Work around the ring with the straight saw, cutting off the little lion slices.

150

neck (Illus. 162). A slice at a time, set the lion upside down in the jaws of a muffled vise and use the coping saw to cut away the small U-shaped pieces of the between-the-leg waste. Now, bearing in mind that the legs are somewhat fragile, take the lion in one hand and a knife in the other, and carefully pare away all the sharp edges and corners. Work backwards and forward over the form, swiftly cutting in the details. Carve a step up around the male lion's mane; cut in the eyes, nostrils, and mouth; texture the head, and so on.

When you have finished carving the male and female lions, dab PVA glue on their feet and set them on their stands. Finally, drill out the 1/8"-diameter tail hole in the lions, glue the cord tail in place, and then begin to work on the next animal.

Painting

Clear away any work-surface clutter, vacuum up any wood dust, wipe the lions over with a damp cloth, and set out your brushes and paints.

Start by applying a primer and an undercoat, and then, when the undercoat is dry, apply a ground coat of tawny yellow. Now, take your fine-point brush and a small amount of tawny yellow mixed with a little bit of brown, and highlight the details of the ears and the feet and those in and around the carved mane. Finally, paint the base green and apply a couple of coats of varnish.

Trouble-shooting and Possible Modifications

• If you find removing the faceplate from the mandrel difficult, slide a wood or leather washer on the mandrel prior to fitting the faceplate.

• If the wood cuts up rough, it's likely that your tools need sharpening. After sharpening your tools, if the wood still cuts up rough, then the wood may be damp or ragged-grained. Therefore, always spend some time carefully choosing your wood.

• Make sure, before you switch on the lathe, that your hair is tied back and the tool rest is just clear of the wood. It's a good idea to run down a checklist before switching on the lathe.

• Once you have turned off the rough, stop the lathe and reset the rest so that it is nearer the wood.

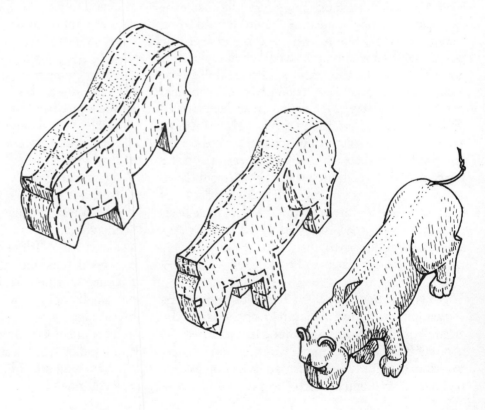

Illus. 162. To make the lioness, chop away the heavy mane (left), reduce the wood around the neck and girth, and clear away the waste from between the legs (middle), and then round off and model the ears and feet (right).

151

Project 5
Ring-Turning a Giraffe in the Cremer Tradition

Design, Structure, and Technique Considerations

Formerly called a camelopard, from the medieval Greek *kamelopardalis*, meaning having a head like a camel and spots like a leopard, the giraffe is our tallest mammal. At about 18 feet high, it really is an unusual beast. Living only in Africa, the giraffe seems to have more than its fair share of problems. For example, it has to spread its legs wide apart and lower its head before it can drink and it is almost mute. And at 18 feet from its toes to its head knobs, the giraffe would either have had to stay out on the top deck of the Ark getting wet, or Noah would have had to cut a trapdoor in one of the between decks for the giraffe's head. Either way, it couldn't have been much fun. Nevertheless, as far as the Cremer Ark makers were concerned, the giraffe was a very popular animal that needed to be included with every Ark.

Now, take a look at Illus. 165 and the drawings showing the ring-turning method, and see how the giraffe's profile relates to the wood being turned. At about 6" from its toes to its nose, and 2" from its chest to its tail, the giraffe needs to be cut from a blank that is about 12" in diameter and 6" thick. Look at all the detailed drawings and see how, at the start of the project, the wood is worked between centers. Study these drawings, make sketches at the museum and zoo, and then make scale drawings, noting the various required techniques.

Tools and Materials

For this project you need:
- a section of small-tree wood that is about 6" thick and 12" in diameter—consider using a clean-cutting knot-free wood, such as lime or holly;
- the use of a lathe;
- a large faceplate;
- faceplate screws and a screwdriver;
- a 4"-thick, 13"-diameter slab of rough wood for the chuck;
- a piece of 1/4"-thick wood for the base;
- a good selection of turning tools, including a couple of side-cutting hook tools;
- a small coping saw;
- a straight saw;
- a couple of whittling knives;
- a hand drill and a small bit;
- an inch, or so, of brown cord;
- PVA glue;

- work-out and tracing paper;
- a measure and callipers;
- a pair of dividers;
- primer and undercoat;
- acrylic paints, in yellow, brown, black, and green;
- varnish;
- broad and fine-point brushes;
- cloths;
- newspaper;
- paint containers;
- scissors; and
- stiff cardboard.

Designing and Cutting the Templates

Take a look at Illus. 165 and see how the giraffe needs to have three templates—one for the head and chest, one for the back, and one for the legs. Consider how the giraffe is to be turned and worked from the rather chunky 12"-diameter blank.

Now, either copying our giraffe or modifying it to suit your own design ideas, draw a strong, bold profile outline and then, with a pencil, press-transfer the traced lines through to your template cardboard. Note how the break lines need to be placed so that the three templates can easily be pushed up against the wood being turned, and then cut out the cardboard forms accordingly. When you have made three templates with break lines at the knees and

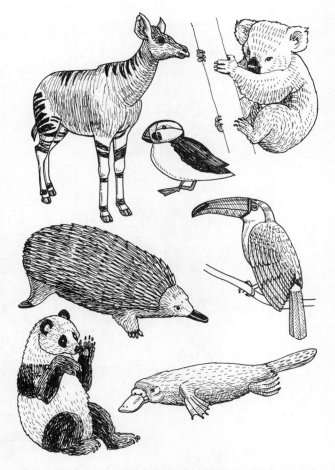

Illus. 164. Inspirational drawing. Looking for other animal oddities? Here are some of our favorites. Top left: African okapi. Middle top: Arctic puffin. Right top: Australian koala bear. Middle left: Australian echidna. Middle right: South American toucan. Bottom left: Asian giant panda. Bottom right: Australian duck-billed platypus.

head, spend a moment or two labelling or color-coding their working faces and mating edges so that they can easily be put back together.

Working Between Centers

When you have made sure that the lathe is in good working order and all of your tools are set out so that they are close at hand, establish center points on both faces of the blank. Note the areas of waste where the screws need to be placed, and then screw

On the following page: Illus. 165. Working drawing. Top: The scale is about four grid squares to 1". Note the form in relation to the ring.

Illus. 163. Project picture. The giraffe is 6" high.

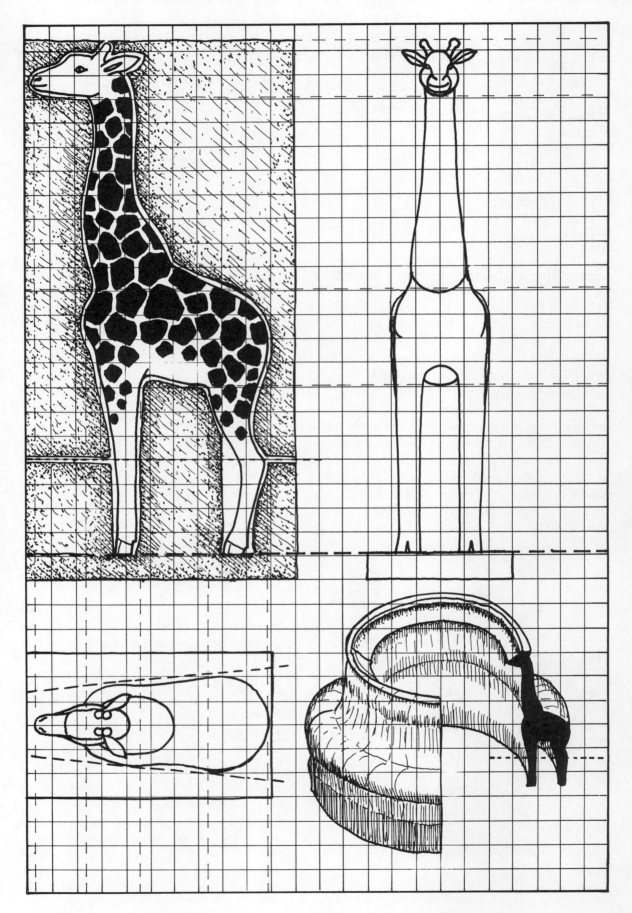

the wood on the faceplate and mount the faceplate on the lathe. Bring up the tailstock and wind the dead center (also called the center point) into the wood until the work is spinning nicely between centers. Ease back the dead center slightly, oil the spin hole, place the T-rest so that it is just clear of the work, and then switch it on.

Working with the tools of your choice (you might use a round-nose chisel), clear away the rough and bring the outside of the ring to a good shape. In other words, swiftly clear away the bulk of the rough from along the whole length of the giraffe's back, and then spend some time bringing the area from the feet to the tail to a good fit and finish. Make checks with the callipers and templates (Illus. 166).

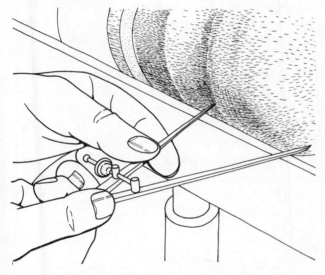

Illus. 166. Secure the blank between the faceplate and center, and then turn off the back waste. Use the callipers to check the size.

Hollowing Out

With the lathe switched off and the wood still mounted on the faceplate, slide the whole tailstock unit back out of the way and reposition the tool rest so that it is as near as possible to the face being turned (Illus. 167). Now, with the round-nose chisel and one of the side-cutting tools, bore out the various inside hollows. Start by turning out the little hollow of the between-the-leg waste, meaning the waste between the giraffe's back and front legs. Carefully work deeper and deeper into the wood

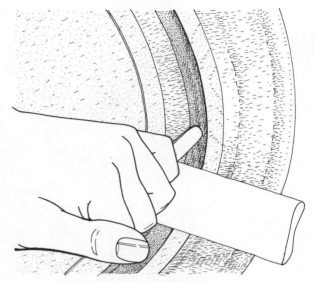

Illus. 167. Slide the tailstock out of the way and hollow-turn the between-the-leg waste.

until the between-the-legs template is a good fit. Continue hollowing out the wood this way until you have shaped the between-the-leg outer-ring profile and the area of deep central waste.

Of course, as the hollows get deeper, you will have to bring the tool rest closer and closer to the work until, finally, the arm of the rest is well into the hole. Although it's tricky, you shouldn't have any problem, as long as you work slowly and carefully, all the while checking with the templates, making sure that the tool rest is clear of the work, and generally being cautious. Finally, when the templates are a good fit, bring the giraffe's legs to a good finish, and take the workpiece off the lathe.

Chuck Work

Screw the blank of chuck wood on the faceplate, mount the faceplate on the lathe, and then swiftly turn out a tapered sinking, into which you can push the legs of the giraffe ring. Now, with the giraffe ring being held tightly and securely in the chuck, take the round-nose chisel and proceed to lower and hollow out the workpiece at its center (Illus. 168).

Once you have pierced the wood and can identify the parts of the giraffe that you have already taken to a good finish, then, with the callipers and templates, gradually open out the center of the ring and work the rest of the profile. This part of the project

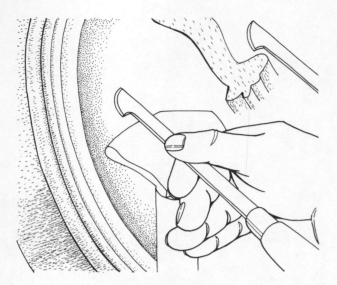

Illus. 168. With the leg side of the ring a good secure fit in the wooden chuck, use one of your shaped gouges to turn off the contours. Work with care and caution.

tends to be difficult because you are trying to turn deeper and deeper into the wood. It's best to take it slowly, working with the arm of the tool rest as close as possible to the wood being turned, and making sure that the tools are kept sharp. Finally, when the ring is finished, ease it out of the chuck and check the section profile by encircling it with the templates.

Cutting and Carving

When you have achieved a good giraffe ring, place it feet-side up on your work surface, set the dividers at about 1¼", and work around the outer back-of-the-legs circumference, striking off arcs. Now, take the straight saw and carefully work around the ring, sawing off giraffe-wedge slices. Try, as you are cutting the slices, to line up the saw blade so that it not only passes through one of the outer-ring step-off arcs, but also through what you estimate to be the dead center of the ring. Allowing for a certain amount of wastage, plan on cutting about 28 giraffe slices.

As to what you should do with the 25, or so, giraffe slices that you don't need for this particular Ark, it's a problem, especially since it's not so easy to remodel a giraffe into another animal. Certainly, you can turn one or two of the slices into okapis

(Illus. 164), but as to the rest, have you ever thought of going into the Ark-making business?

Now, secure the giraffe slices, a piece at a time, upside down in the jaws of a muffled vise and start to cut away the between-the-leg waste (Illus. 169). Use the straight saw to make an initial tail-to-chest center-line pilot cut; then work the rest of the waste by taking the coping saw and sawing down the line of the inside leg and into the bottom of the pilot cut. When this is done, clear away all your large tools and refresh your eye by taking another look at Illus. 163 and 165 and at any drawings from the museum or zoo that you might have made.

Now, take a sharp knife and work swiftly over the sawn profiles, removing all the angles and edges. As you are whittling away, watch out so that you don't run the knife into the grain and thus split the wood. Using a razor-sharp knife and working with care and caution, try to remove only the finest wispy slivers. Round off the legs, shape the beautiful long neck, carve the head knobs, and make all the other features that go into making up the giraffe. As with the other projects, as you are carving, try to relate to the run of the grain. When the giraffe is finished, run your fingertips over its form. If you find any rough imperfections, eliminate them with the knife and/or a scrap of sandpaper. Finally, glue the giraffe to its ¼"-thick base and put it to one side.

Painting and Finishing

Take a look at the giraffes in the color section on page D, and see how we have used a yellow ground, or base, color and then blocked in the islands of pattern with dark brown. Note the size and placement of the brown patches. For example, on the large body areas the patches are large, and then as they occur down the legs towards the feet, and up the neck towards the head, they become smaller and finer and lighter in color. In fact, by the time the pattern reaches the extremities, it fades out, leaving the giraffe's nose, ears, and feet a pale buff-yellow.

Having made sure that your work area is free from dust and debris, wipe the giraffe over with a damp cloth and set out your paints and brushes. When this is done, brush on a primer and then, allowing the paints to dry out between coats, apply an undercoat

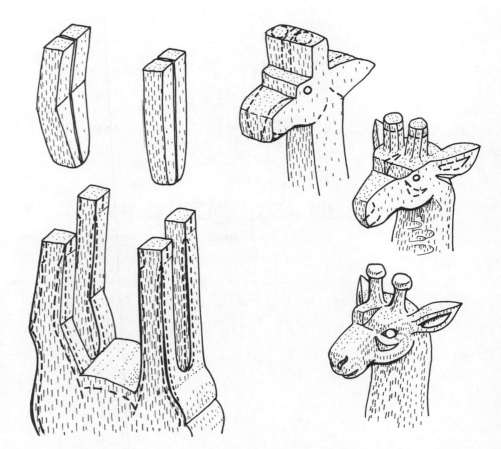

Illus. 169. Left: Cut away the between-the-leg waste. Top middle: Identify the forms and draw in the basic stop cuts. Right: Chop away the waste. Bottom right: Use a fine knife to achieve the final modelling.

and a yellow top coat. When the paint is dry, take a soft pencil and, starting on the large body area, draw in the patches. Noting how the brown patches are basically rounded, and how the yellow "roads" that run around the patches stay at a constant width, take a fine-point brush and a little nonrunny brown paint and carefully go over the form, blocking in the pencil-drawn areas. While you are waiting for the brown paint to dry, highlight the black and/or brown eyes and nose, and paint the base green. Finally, drill the tail hole, glue and plug the cord tail, and apply a couple of generous coats of varnish.

Troubleshooting and Possible Modifications

• Prior to switching on the lathe, make sure that

your working environment is generally safe. The floor should be clear of clutter, you should be wearing shoes that won't slip, and the tool rest should be clear of the workpiece. Also, it's best to wear safety glasses or a visor.

• Since the giraffe ring needs to fit firmly in the wooden chuck, make sure that the hole, or recess, is tapered. If you are concerned about the ring being thrown out of the spinning chuck, drill a hole through the sides of the chuck—meaning a hole that just skims the side of the giraffe ring—and tap in a wedge peg.

• If you want to achieve a worn, handled antique effect, after the paint is dry rub the workpiece with fine sandpaper, apply a coat of varnish "crackle," and finally rub a little bit of dry brown paint in the crackle patina.

METRIC EQUIVALENCY CHART
mm—millimetres   cm—centimetres
INCHES TO MILLIMETRES AND CENTIMETRES

inches	mm	cm	inches	cm	inches	cm
⅛	3	0.3	9	22.9	30	76.2
¼	6	0.6	10	25.4	31	78.7
⅜	10	1.0	11	27.9	32	81.3
½	13	1.3	12	30.5	33	83.8
⅝	16	1.6	13	33.0	34	86.4
¾	19	1.9	14	35.6	35	88.9
⅞	22	2.2	15	38.1	36	91.4
1	25	2.5	16	40.6	37	94.0
1¼	32	3.2	17	43.2	38	96.5
1½	38	3.8	18	45.7	39	99.1
1¾	44	4.4	19	48.3	40	101.6
2	51	5.1	20	50.8	41	104.1
2½	64	6.4	21	53.3	42	106.7
3	76	7.6	22	55.9	43	109.2
3½	89	8.9	23	58.4	44	111.8
4	102	10.2	24	61.0	45	114.3
4½	114	11.4	25	63.5	46	116.8
5	127	12.7	26	66.0	47	119.4
6	152	15.2	27	68.6	48	121.9
7	178	17.8	28	71.1	49	124.5
8	203	20.3	29	73.7	50	127.0

Index